How to Retire Remarkably Early
OPERATION
ENOUGH!

How to Retire Remarkably Early
OPERATION ENOUGH!

ANITA DHAKE

Copyright © 2017 by Anita Dhake

All rights reserved. No part of this publication may be reproduced, distributed, or transmitted in any form or by any means, including photocopying, recording, or other electronic or mechanical methods, without the prior written permission of the publisher, except in the case of brief quotations embodied in critical reviews and certain other noncommercial uses permitted by copyright law. For permission requests, write to the publisher, addressed "Attention: Permissions Coordinator," at the email address below.

The Power of Publishing
www.thepowerofpublishing.com
thepowerofpublishing@gmail.com

Ordering Information:
Quantity sales. Special discounts are available on quantity purchases by corporations, associations, and others. For details, contact the publisher at the email address above.

Printed in the United States of America

Publisher's Cataloging-in-Publication data
Dhake, Anita.
Operation Enough! : How to Retire Remarkably Early / Anita Dhake
p. cm.
ISBN 978-0-9992336-0-3
1. Self Help 2. Happiness. 3. Financial Independence
LCN 2017912992

First Edition

ISBN 978-0-9992336-0-3 (paperback)
ISBN 978-0-9992336-1-0 (e-book)

10 9 8 7 6 5 4 3 2 1

To you, my dear reader. Without you, this is nothing.

And my mom. Hi, Mom!

CONTENTS

Preface ix
My Life Bucket List xi
Introduction xv
Chapter 1: What Exactly Is Enough? 1
    Action Plan! Where do you want to go? 17
Chapter 2: How Should I Spend My Money? 19
    First, buy security. This is always first. 20
    Spend money on what you repeatedly do 29
    Buy the ability to say yes to adventure and friendship 33
    Action Plan! How do you use money's superpowers currently? 43
Chapter 3: How Do I Save? 47
    Where are you? 47
    Action Plan! Where are you? 51
    Don't buy stuff 55
    How should you shop? 57
    Case study: a television 66
    Buy used 75
    Sell what you don't need 78

    What makes your financial avatar smile? 87

    How do you hold yourself accountable? 99

    Do you advocate for yourself? 109

    Action Plan! Plan your calendar 117

Chapter 4: How Should I Invest? 119

    Do you know about compound interest? Are you using it correctly? 119

    How will you know when you have enough? 129

    Action Plan! Plot away 143

    What about Real Property? 143

Chapter 5: How Should I Not Spend My Money? 155

Chapter 6: Still Skeptical? 197

List of lists 205

Acknowledgments 211

Books you should read 213

References 215

About the Author 219

PREFACE

Hello dear reader. Thanks for reading. I wrote this book to cross off item #6 on my Life Bucket List—write a book. I decided to write about retiring early—item #7—because I retired at thirty-three and people seem rather interested in that fact.

Maybe you are one of those people.

I also wrote this book to lay flowers at the feet of my spiritual masters—books, generally, and *Your Money or Your Life*, specifically. Books are powerful. A book can change your life if you're ready to hear the message. If you're ready to hear the message, I'll show you what life can be when you have enough money to do what you want.

MY LIFE BUCKET LIST

1. See the world
2. ~~Learn to swim~~
3. Learn to cook like Mom
4. ~~Get in shape enough to hike the Grand Canyon~~
5. Hike the Grand Canyon
6. ~~Write a book~~
7. ~~Retire early~~
8. Learn a foreign language
9. ~~Feel at home in a foreign country (live abroad for at least six months)~~
10. ~~Fall recklessly in love~~
11. ~~Start a business~~
12. Start a nonprofit
13. ~~Make a positive, lasting difference for fifty people~~
14. Solve a problem for the future
15. ~~Be on TV once~~
16. Be a writer
17. Get a six-pack (abs)

18. Maintain the six-pack abs for a year
19. ~~Get an advanced degree~~
20. See the northern lights
21. Be an extra on a television show or movie
22. ~~Have a job I really enjoy~~
23. Go skiing
24. ~~Go bungee jumping~~
25. ~~Jump out of an airplane~~
26. Go hang gliding or paragliding. One of the glidings.
27. Work in a factory
28. ~~Work as a waitress~~
29. Keep chickens so I can gather fresh eggs
30. Read a book a day for a year
31. Age gracefully
32. Go on a book tour
33. Take a vow of silence
34. Find a fossil
35. Be a teetotaler
36. Learn to sew
37. Learn woodworking
38. Go scuba diving
39. Live in New York City once, but leave before it makes me hard*
40. Live in Northern California once, but leave before it makes me soft*
41. Be generous

42. Learn to dance
43. Fall responsibly in love
44. Go on a long bike road trip

*Instructions from *Wear Sunscreen: A Primer for Real Life* by Mary Schmich

INTRODUCTION

I'm Anita. Hi. What can I tell you about myself? At the time of this typing, I have completed thirty-four laps around our glorious sun. I travel a lot (fifty-six countries so far) and read even more. I set grand goals for myself and give them delightful operational nicknames, cackling in delight if I achieve them.

This is the story of *Operation Enough!*—my quest to retire as soon as I possibly could, to cackle mercilessly at my alarm clock each morning. As you'll see, it has worked quite well, I think. I cackle quite regularly.

Let me give you my credentials with a quick rundown of my financial life to date. I'll be the first to admit that I was lucky. I grew up in the Midwestern United States to immigrant parents from India. The youngest of three daughters, I was fortunate enough to be born in the "right" generation in the cycle of wealth—a vantage point from which I could clearly see the value of money, but not the struggle to subsist or the eventual squander and entitlement.

I'm also lucky that I'm a fast reader and that my spot in the universe granted me easy access to libraries. When I was a teenager, I read the financial self-help book *Your Money or Your Life: 9 Steps to Transforming Your Relationship with Money and Achieving Financial Independence* by Vicki Robin and Joe Dominguez, which encapsulates the attitude toward money that made sense to me. Enough is enough. Choose living your life over accumulating money for accumulation's sake. Inspired, I added *retire early* to my Life Bucket List.

At twenty, I graduated from the University of Illinois at Urbana-Champaign with a degree in economics. I went to work for an insurance company in a suburb outside Chicago as a workers' compensation claims-handler with a starting salary of $40,000 per year and perhaps $15,000 in student loans.

At this point, I went off the rails, drifting without any clear goals. I knew to avoid credit card debt and to put as much money as the government would allow into my 401(k) retirement account, but not much else. I saved whatever excess accumulated in a checking account and paid the minimum on my student loans.

Getting an advanced degree was on my Life Bucket List, too, so at twenty-three, I started law school at the University of Chicago. I'm lucky when it comes to those standardized tests. After my first year, my school hosted on-campus interviewing. Law firms came and wooed us with promises of large salaries and glamorous lives. Big Law, they called it.

While chatting with a law school friend, I laid out a premise. If we made four times what the average person made, could we not retire four times earlier?

"No," he responded.

Apparently this wasn't as obvious to him.

But the seed from my teenage years started to sprout. I reread *Your Money or Your Life*. Ideas swirled.

If I started working in Chicago instead of New York or California, the places most of my classmates sought, I could keep my expenses low. Chicago was a big enough city to offer the Big Law starting salary ($160,000), but the numbers on life's price tags were more reasonable.

Operation Enough! began to form.

Plan in hand, right before I started my last year of law school, I joined a large law firm in Chicago as a summer associate. After that stint ended, they extended an offer for me to start working full time upon graduation the following year. What luck!

Life was going according to plan, dear reader.

And then Lehman Brothers, a major player in the global economy, decided to collapse. Everyone started panicking. Fire and brimstone. The whole deal. Recession! At least that's what the news told me. I shrugged and went on with my life.

A few months before graduation, my law firm reached out to me. They were still trying to put out the fire and move the brimstone and didn't really have much work for new associates. They knew I would be bored coming into the office every day just to play FreeCell, so they offered me a third of my salary to go do whatever I wanted for a bit. Oh, they also offered to pay my minimum student loan payments for a year. And, of course, they would still pay for me to take the bar exam and loan me money for living expenses for the summer while I took the bar.

Giddy, I accepted. $77,000 and a year of freedom? Um, yeah! I told you I was lucky.

In June 2009 I graduated law school at the age of twenty-six with a badge on my resume that seemed to impress people and six figures of student loan debt. I threw some of my deferral money at my loans, but the rest I spent wandering the globe and cackling in delight.

Control. Autonomy. Sweet, sweet freedom.

To debt freedom and dancing a jig

Finally, in October 2010, I started my career as a corporate lawyer. At that point, I owed roughly $95,000 for that privilege. Oof.

I decided to think of paying off that debt as a game. A

game I could win. A game I could kick the banks' ass at. Some of my loans—$10,000 from my law firm and $5,000 from my sister—carried a 0% interest rate. The rest came from banks. Banks who were positively drooling at the prospect of all the interest I agreed to pay them. I understood the fine print, though. If I wanted to pay them earlier, they had to accept. Giving the banks as little of my money as possible became the focus of my everything. I dubbed this new project *Operation Get Rid of that Debt, Man*.

I'm lucky that I'm really good at coming up with operation names.

Finally I put my long-simmering plan into action. In Chicago, I could afford a sunny two-bedroom, two-and-a-half-bathroom apartment for $1,500 per month. That's less than half what I would have paid in Los Angeles or New York for more space. By getting a roommate, I cut that down to $750 per month and split all the utilities. The delightful roommate also came with a lot of furniture and a lasting friendship.

I rode public transportation, biked, or walked everywhere. The aforementioned apartment's location was nothing short of ideal. Seventeen minutes via the blue line ($80/month) or twenty minutes biking (free) brought me to my office.

With shelter and commuting covered, I looked for

other ways to save. My two older sisters with professional jobs and similar figures gifted me some of their old clothes. Their hand-me-downs populated most of my wardrobe, and the few pieces I bought that first year totaled maybe $100.

I brought my breakfast and lunch to work most days. I went out to eat and for drinks with my friends for my sanity, but never more than once or twice a week. When I worked late, my firm paid for my dinner and a cab home. The firm also offered a free gym with free personal trainers. Glamorous life, indeed. I put my favorite form of entertainment (traveling) on hiatus. No movies, music, or books made their way onto my credit cards.

I woke up chanting the number I had left to pay and went to bed counting down the days to the next payday. I prioritized paying off the loans with the highest interest rate and paying back my sister. Up to 85% of my net income went towards this operation. My bonus, my tax return, the quarter I found on the street—every extra cent went to maximizing that percentage.

You could have called me obsessed, and I'd just nod in agreement. I calculated and recalculated payoff dates and how much less interest the bank would receive from me. I celebrated each time I eliminated a loan.

In October 2011, I nearly emptied out my bank account and spent my emergency fund to pay off my last student loan. One year and two days after I started my legal career, I declared myself officially debt-free and danced a little jig. My stressful job became instantly more tolerable. I no longer feared the time when my law firm would realize that I was an imposter and fire me.

Now let's retire
Life loosened a bit after that. I spent money on travel again. Occasionally, I purchased expensive coconut water. I lost my roommate to a new neighborhood and decided I could afford to live alone.

When I was within shouting distance of retiring, my law firm asked if I wanted to hang out in their Sydney office for a while.

What? Trade my wonderfully inexpensive Chicago for a city that would smack me with a daily dose of sticker shock? The rent alone would double my expenses. I checked.

Of course I quickly accepted. Because here's the thing: money is an ally and a tool to help you live your life the way you want. You have to know yourself well enough to know what you want and what will make you happy. "Feel at home in a foreign country" claimed Life Bucket List spot number nine, so I decided to put the "retire early" dream down and play with the "live abroad" one for a bit.

I moved to Sydney in January 2014 at the age of thirty-one. Decadence ruled my time there. In a city with high rents, I paid for an apartment with an extra bedroom that sat mostly empty. I ate out quite a bit and rarely cooked. My bike sat parked, forsaken and sad, while I took cabs all over town. I justified these conveniences in the moment by imagining the income line in my charts.

Looking back through my old journals now, I realize that those Sydney extravagances did not add up to any increased happiness. My favorite part of the day used to be biking to and from work in Chicago. "Learn to cook like Mom" graces a top ten spot on my Life Bucket List, but utilizing that skill took a back seat when I finished law school. I felt only mockery when I looked at my empty extra bedroom.

Since I knew Sydney was a limited-time gig and because I'm human, I shrugged off the larger expenses. Despite these increased costs, I still lived well below my means and saved an average of more than 76% of each paycheck.

And then! When my temporary relocation ended in October 2015, instead of going back to the Chicago office, I quit my job, ditched most of my stuff, and started to wander the world. In short, I retired. I had just turned thirty-three. Once I no longer had to pay Sydney's rent, my average monthly expenses were lower than my projected monthly passive income from investments.

That's *Operation Enough!* Save enough money to live

the life you want without wasting too much of your life doing something you don't love to earn it.

I know that I made more money than the average bear when I was working as a lawyer and that luck attached itself to me, but I hope you don't dismiss my advice because of those facts. Nobody is going to be in your exact same situation. By sharing what's worked for me, I hope you will think about your own life and experiment with your own finances and decide what works for you and what doesn't.

Do you want to do your own *Operation Enough!*? I can tell you what I did and what I think you should do.

The rest of this book is organized around five questions to ponder:
1. What exactly is enough?
2. How should I spend money?
3. How do I save money?
4. How should I invest?
5. How should I *not* spend money?

I've also designed some action plans to help you apply the lessons from my own early retirement to yours. Hopefully this encouragement from me slips you into the right frame of mind. Maybe you won't be able to pay off your debt or retire as quickly as I did, but so what? We had different starting points and Lady Luck has graced us in different ways. I'm guessing that you're about as talented as I am. I'm not extraordinary. I have no idea what I'm doing. I take from other people's ideas and experiment to see what works for me. This is what worked for me.

And it really worked. It could work for you too.

CHAPTER 1

What Exactly Is Enough?

Do you have enough money to be happy?

If you're grinning and nodding, then hooray! No need to read further. Let's fist bump and make explosion noises, maybe take a walk. Once money no longer occupies much of your brain space, you can concentrate on other shit. **The most valuable thing money can buy is freedom from worrying about money.** Not needing money is better than money itself. Obvious, right?

If you *weren't* fist bumping me, well, that's a bummer. A major bummer. I can't even begin to tell you how much easier and happier life is when you have enough.

I'll try though. Enough is awesome. Enough is the ability to design your own life.

With enough, you take complete control of your own story. Use your time to do whatever you want whenever you darn well feel like doing it. Your time is the one thing you can't pawn off on somebody else. What do you want to be doing? Are you doing it?

With enough, you get to hang out with your family and your friends and your pets and build these awesome, fulfilling relationships. Humans are social creatures and we freaking love hanging out with other human beings. You get to choose your people when you have enough.

With enough, you can pursue your passion and make your mark on the world. Humans yearn to leave a legacy. Are you doing what you're meant to do? If you have no idea what you're meant to do, having enough means time to find out.

So, what's enough to make you happy? Have you ever actually thought about it?

Seriously. How much money do you need to be rich? Surely if you were a billionaire, you'd be rich. What about a millionaire? What about someone who has $756,715.85? That's equivalent to $1,000,000 Australian dollars, converted from US dollars in January 2017. If you fiddle with the exchange rates, you're probably a millionaire somewhere in the world.

Which final penny makes someone wealthy? How much is enough?

I'm not the first person to contemplate this question.

This is the ancient sorites paradox, or the argument of the growing heap. When does a pile become a heap? I think it's a heap when you can look at the pile and be all like "Yup, that's definitely a heap." It's a *feeling*.

Okay, that's not satisfying in the least. This is why I studied economics and law instead of philosophy at school. Yes, it's a feeling, but it can also be a real number. A number you get to decide.

I added *retire early* to my Life Bucket List as a teenager. Rather than quibble over the definition of "retire," I quantified this Bucket List item as "generate enough passive income to cover my expenses." I plot those two numbers on a chart regularly and smile evilly. My diabolical plan is working! I have enough money to be happy.

I'll explain the chart in more detail later, but theoretically, this means I don't have to use my brain juice to earn more money. I know I have enough because I have a pretty chart that tells me so.

One of the many, many reasons I love my chart is because it shows me how much is enough *for me*. That is a powerful bit of knowledge. Everyone has a different amount at which they no longer need additional money, a point where they consider themselves rich.

I feel rich because I have enough. Your enough will be different from my enough, which will be different from that guy over there's enough. **But the less you need, the sooner you will feel rich.**

Money itself stops being meaningful after a while. It's like going apple picking. Yeah, maybe the first few apples are delicious, but how many can you digest? At some point, that extra dollar is kind of pointless. Living just to earn means wasting life. You can't eat all those apples. They'll go bad before you can finish them, and who has enough time and freezer and pantry space for canning? Why waste your time picking them? Why not go for a hayride instead?

I think this metaphor is breaking down. In real life, I would eat none of the apples because I'm allergic. But you get my point.

Maybe you've heard that money can't buy happiness, but that's a lie. Money can buy happiness if you know what to buy. The problem is that we have too many choices and so much temptation. Quite often, we make the wrong choice.

Think about our lives for a second. We get up when the alarm clock yells at us, get dressed in clothes that we buy for work, drive through traffic in a car that we are still paying for—all to work at the job we need to pay for the clothes and the clock and the car, and the house we leave vacant all day.[*]

I don't think it has to be that way, and I've done every-

---

[*] Most of that sentence is a mangled version of a quote from journalist Ellen Goodman.

thing in my power to design my life so that I have enough money to *not* live that way. You can too.

Instead of thinking about money, just do…anything else. Personally, I like to spend my time reading, writing, traveling, planning, seeing friends and family, and being in constant awe that I get to live this life. I work on my various Life Bucket List items. I sleep in.

Of course, your retirement won't be exactly the same as my retirement. That would be creepy. You have to figure out what brings you joy and spend money on *that*.

Personal finance is easy. Don't spend money on crap you personally and specifically don't need for happiness. The hard part is knowing yourself well enough to know what that might be. It's the "personal" part of personal finance that trips most people up. Myself included! What's fun for one person might be boring as sin for the dude sitting next to him yawning.

Know yourself.

I've noticed that most people who are unhappy with their money life fall into one of the categories below.

Category 1: You don't have enough money to be happy because you're teetering precariously on the edge of disaster, scraping by and often worrying about the basic necessities. All of your energy is focused on how to make it to the end of the month before you run out of money.

The people in this category are too exhausted from the effort of existence to be reading this, so I'm guessing that's not you. This is poverty—an issue which I am in no way qualified to address.

Category 2: You don't have enough money to be happy because money is scary. You keep your head buried in the sand about your finances and feel anxious only when you allow yourself to think about it. Which is never. You don't know where you stand. You don't want to know. You're keen to go do something else, anything else.

The people in this category are actively avoiding books like this, so that's definitely not you. I should have written that in the third person.

Category 3: You don't have enough money to be happy because no amount of money can make you happy. All you know is that you need more. You peer at what everyone else just bought and think happiness is in keeping up. Your entire personality and sense of worth is based on how much money you make. You're addicted to money.

If you're in this category, you drive me a little nuts. You're on third base! Just run home. Your status as a high-earner means you *could* do your own *Operation Enough!*

stupidly fast. I'm not equipped to deal with addiction, but keep reading. I'm not done trying to persuade you.

Category 4: You don't have enough money to be happy because you still feel compelled to work a job that doesn't fill your heart with purpose. You want to do something else, but you don't have enough money yet. You're not teetering like the people in category one, but you would concede that an unexpected bill's arrival in the mail would require a deep breath. You know the basics of money management—spend less than you earn, avoid credit card debt, invest somehow at some point—but knowing it and actually doing it are two very different things.

If that's you, I think some of my babbling might help. I'm guessing you're not using money's superpowers correctly. And yes, there is absolutely a correct way to use money and an incorrect way. Just as there is an incorrect and correct way to use Superman.

Correct usage: "Superman! A meteor just flew into the engine of my plane! Eek! Can you fly up and save me from this plummeting death trap?"
Incorrect usage: "Superman! Can you clean my bathtub?"

The incorrect usage would make a terrible movie.

And using money's superpowers incorrectly means you're making terrible financial decisions.

I know it's tough to see the forest for the trees and that your day-to-day financial decisions are easy to justify in the moment.

Let me show you what I do to examine my own financial decisions. It's silly, but kind of fun and enormously helpful for me. Because I'm a simpleton and easily delighted, I like to personify money concepts and imagine everything as a comic book.

The main character and protagonist in my comic book scenario is me, or rather my financial avatar. Her name is Mimi. Your main character will be you. A cartoonier version of yourself, rather.

If you have debt, I imagine your financial avatar as a baby who is always screaming. He requires constant vigilance and attention. If you're not in debt, but still beholden to a job that you don't like, the avatar is a kid. You can leave him home alone, but not overnight. If you don't have enough because nothing is enough, your avatar is a bratty teenager who talks back and makes you want to smack him. When you have enough money to be happy, the avatar is an adult. A responsible and self-sufficient adult that lives on the other side of town. You schedule lunch once every four months to catch up and occasionally text each other funny cat pictures.

I don't know about you, but I like having my financial avatar as a texting buddy.

There are other characters in this comic book, too. Mimi is good friends with John Cash, a Superman-like creature in my financial avatar world.

He secures everything Mimi needs without hesitation and with the occasional martini. He shares wisdom, saves her from plane crashes, and gives her the time she needs to read books. He uses his influence to make her life easier. John Cash is an indispensable friend.

This is how you want to interact with money. As a friend. A tool. John Cash will happily sew up your parachute, umbrella, and safety net while you take a nap. He lets you react the way you want to react and, presumably, put your own self-interest first. He gives you the freedom to make your life what you want it to be. Having cash as servant simply means having *enough*.

The villain in my comic imagination comes in the form of Ms. Cash. Ms. Cash is John Cash's twin sister, but she's a bit of a bully. While John likes to serve, Ms. Cash likes to demand.

When she latches onto you, she taunts you, mocks you, and sows stress and discontent. She gloats in your ear that you have no control, that you're living on the edge of broke, that you don't have *enough*, and that whatever you do have is so much worse than what other people have.

Ms. Cash doesn't hold the door open for you when you're literally right behind her. She's just a horrible person.

This is how you *don't* want to interact with money. Ms. Cash reminds you that you're one slip away from disaster and urges you to make yourself feel better with any easy pleasure you can find RIGHT NOW. She has the power and she never lets you forget it.

How you perceive money—as John Cash or Ms. Cash—is determined by your attitude more than your income. Most of the anxiety people feel about money comes from their perceived lack of control over it.

You have more control than you realize because you have complete control over your attitude.

Check your attitude

Money isn't inherently good or bad. You make it good or bad with your attitude and your purchases. Money as master evokes fear, stress, and discontent. Money as servant is just a cool guy happy to help. Make it your master and you'll be miserable. Make it your servant and you might still be miserable, but it won't be because of money.

Attitude makes all the difference. I'm assuming you have the right attitude because you're reading this book. Part of having the right attitude is being the type of person who actively plots and ponders how to make things better.

What pathway does your brain take when confronted

with a challenge? Do you try to solve the problem or do you whine about it? Are you waiting for someone to take care of you? Are you looking for ways to dismiss me because of my luck? Or are you looking for ways to inspire yourself?

A feeling of control over your life is vital to happiness. I know that control is an illusion and that the universe might accidentally knock down anyone with the hubris to think otherwise, but I also know that feeling completely out of control really drags me down. The way I tackle everything is by thinking and focusing on my axis of control. The axis of control is based on the serenity prayer and involves splitting everything in life into three categories.

God, grant me the serenity to accept the things I cannot change…

Category one includes anything I possess exactly zero control over. Negative control if that's possible. The sun will rise in the sky every morning whether I would prefer it to or not.

What's your attitude towards this fact? A counterproductive attitude involves angry muttering and stewing. The ideal attitude involves relief: The world is too full of things! You'd go mad if you had to control everything!

I'll give you an example. As Ben Franklin once told me, "Nothing can be said to be certain, except death and taxes." Since this is a money book, I'm only here to cheer you up about taxes. You have to pay taxes. How do you feel about that? Can you find a way to not feel bummed?

I invented a character for Mimi to interact with to ease my convulsions from looking at the taxes lines of my paychecks. He's a gentleman named Mayor Civil.

Mayor Civil buys Mimi the luxuries of civilization. He pays for the bike lanes and the police. He funds the justice system and the parks. Through public schools, he trains Mimi's future employees. Most importantly of all, he runs the library—the happiest place in the world.

Mimi likes him. Well, she likes him most of the time, anyway. He can be rude, and she suspects he occasionally spends her money on his cuff links.

Taxes are the price you pay to live in a civilization. And since I freaking love living in civilization, I try to consider it a bargain.

...The courage to change the things I can... (Still talking to God here.)

Category two of the axis of control includes the universe

of things I have complete control over. My attitude. My interpretations. How I spend cash. Trying to find an activity that delights me. But especially my attitude.

If your attitude towards early retirement is that it's impossible, then it will be impossible. For you.

Adjust your attitude from "I can't" to "How can I?" and the part of your brain that thinks will begin to focus on that. It's what your brain is for. Thinking about whatever you ask it to think about.

This category is where you should put all your energy. What can you do? Courage up and go do it! Don't buy that thing you don't need. Ask for a raise. Make some goals and mark your progress. Create a spreadsheet. Pretty soon, the problem becomes manageable. Because you're managing it!

...And the wisdom to know the difference.

Category three of the axis of control includes things I have *some* control over. How well I succeed at the activity that delights me. How much money I make. The way I position myself for the inevitable bad. How much wiggle room I give myself.

Life is going to throw shit at you occasionally. You don't have control over what or when the shit comes, but you can give yourself cushion. Wisdom means working on the things you can control so you're not flattened by the things you can't.

Check in on your attitude. Do you believe that you have

some control over doing better? That's vital. That's first and foremost. I can't control everything, but I can control my attitude. I can feel as in control as I want to be. There's the T-shirt line.

ACTION PLAN!
WHERE DO YOU WANT TO GO?

LET'S PLAN YOUR own *Operation Enough!* so you can have enough money to be happy. Take a moment and ask yourself where you want to go. Pull out your hopes and your pen and your brain cells and imagine the best possible life for yourself. Visualize your ideal retirement.

Ask yourself some questions and seriously answer them:
1. What would a day in your retirement look like?
2. How do you want the story of your life to read?
3. What would you put on your Life Bucket List?

Consider what it means to have enough and work toward that enough. We'll be bumping our fists in celebration before too long.

CHAPTER 2

How Should I Spend My Money?

MONEY CAN BUY you happiness if you buy the right things and make the right choices. Here is what you need to be happy according to ancient philosophers, many studies and, most importantly, my own experience.

1. A sense of security
2. A feeling of control over your decisions
3. Purpose and progress in your endeavors
4. Pleasant interactions and good relationships with your friends and family

If you have enough money to buy all these things and then you proceed to buy all these things, happiness follows. That's *Operation Enough!*—having enough money to pursue happiness. Do what you want. Commandeer more of your brain cells for other stuff. It's great!

So how do you do it? I don't know exactly what you know already, so I'm going to start with the basics. Hopefully, you'll be nodding along for this next part.

First, buy security. This is always first.

There aren't a lot of hard and fast rules, but this is definitely one of those hard and fast rules. Worship the wiggle room and buy your security.

Security consists of four components: (a) a happy place to lay your head at night; (b) enough good, nutritious food to eat consistently and without worry; (c) your health and well-being; and (d) the ability to squeeze life's lemons and make the most out of a bad situation.

These come before everything else. Everything. But they especially come before stuff.

Buy a roof over your head and food for your stomach

You need a spot where you feel comfortable and safe. Shelter, housing, accommodations, home. Whatever you want to call it.

You also need enough good, healthy food to eat consistently.

I was born in a lucky spot in the universe and I have

never had to think about these two items. You probably were too. As a citizen of the United States, I have complete freedom of movement and choice of where I live. Nearly every conceivable cost of living exists in the United States. If rent and such take up too much of your earnings, dozens of other cities will welcome your contribution to maintaining civilization. And compared to Europe, everyone speaks the same language! Take that, Europe!

When you stop to smell the roses for a second, you begin to realize how charmed you are. You're reading this. You don't just subsist. That's more than a shocking percentage of the world can say. You have options.

The basic necessities that a human being requires to survive are available with amazing abundance. Technology and civilization have combined to create a world whose people don't need to spend all their energy on survival.

What's your attitude about your current food and shelter situation?

Ms. Cash will point out that your boss has a chandelier and eats sushi for lunch. John Cash will delight at the roof over your head and the fact that you're not hungry. Ms. Cash tells you it's hopeless while John Cash brainstorms. Who would you rather be friends with?

It's all relative. Expand your circle and compare your situation to the entire universe to realize how much control you start with. People in other countries risk their lives for access to the necessities most of us take for granted. North Korea, for example, serves as a terrifyingly, hauntingly, stupidly good reminder that the universe really adores you.

Buy your health
Spend money freely on your health. Health is like money. You notice it when it's not there. Just being healthy or just being wealthy can't make you happy, but being unhealthy and unwealthy can certainly make you unhappy.

It's cheaper in the long run to be healthy, so do what you can. Remember that an ounce of prevention is worth a pound of cure. I didn't make that phrase up.

Getting a flu shot lowers your chances of getting the flu. If you never get the flu, that means you don't have to take time off work and lose your hourly wage. If you're salaried or retired, no flu means no wasting time being sick.

Going to the dentist early catches the cavity before it rots through your jaw. That sounds painful. Taking vitamins prevents something or other. I don't think the studies are conclusive.

What I'm trying to say is that it's always cheaper not to have the problem in the first place. It's also cheaper to catch the problem quickly. It's certainly cheaper to manage the problem instead of ignoring it and then getting emergency treatment when it gets overwhelming.

Take care of yourself. Exercise. Eat right. You'll spend less on healthcare if you do. Probably. You'll feel better, too.

In a society where health insurance isn't a basic human right, your best defense is to treat your body as the precious vessel it is.

Maintaining your mental health is another tool in your arsenal. Be nice to yourself. Encourage yourself. Be your own cheerleader. Compassion for yourself is a major piece of the happiness puzzle and such a valuable trait. There are enough people out there who are eager to tear you down and tell you how awful and worthless you are. Why join the chorus? Why not be a voice of calm and tenderness in the deluge?

Research shows that when the voice inside your head is a friend and not a bully, you're more likely to:

1. Try new things because failure doesn't automatically come with scoldings
2. Have more self-confidence
3. Empathize with other people because you understand that everyone fails and everyone struggles
4. Be healthier with better immune response
5. Take care of yourself because you don't want yourself to suffer
6. Accept blame for your mistakes because, again, failure doesn't automatically come with scoldings[1]

"Be nice to yourself" is one of those life tips that seems

so obvious when I write it on my to-do list, but I am shockingly bad at doing on a day-to-day basis. I'm constantly complaining about myself to myself and then complaining to myself that all I ever do is complain.

I see literally zero downside to being nice to yourself. All anybody wants is acceptance and love. I have a rule that I've been implementing with varying degrees of success for years. Don't say anything to yourself that you wouldn't say to a friend of yours. Whenever you do say something mean to yourself, stop and say something nice to counteract the negativity.

I love this bit because it's free! It costs you nothing to create your own inner ally.

Buy wiggle room

Wiggle room is the planning and foundation. It means the ability to handle the universe's annoyances. How quickly can you get up after life hip-checks you? How easy is it to be gritty?

After you have no debt and you start increasing your net worth, your wiggle room grows and grows. Eventually, your wiggle room grows so big, it turns into financial independence.

When I was paying off my student loans, I kept about $4,000 in my checking account for wiggle room. That was about two and a half months of living expenses for me.

During that time, I thought of wiggle room as enough money to avoid Judge Judy's wrath.

"Judge" shows litter the daytime TV landscape, but Judy is by far the best, in my opinion. Watching her dole out justice makes my day. She's good at doling. I also feel like I learn so much about human beings and relationships from her show.

The paltry sums of money people go to court over, prolonging toxic contact with someone who is better left behind and forgotten, shocks me. That's not to say that you should let people take advantage of you, but sometimes it's better to move forward without the hassle, stress, and time of suing for some cash you're owed and chalking the loss up to a lesson learned.

It's good to at least have that option. Wiggle room is that option. Do you have control over who is in your life?

I find the vast majority of failed romantic relationships showcased on *Judge Judy* terribly sad. She hits you? He calls you names? Treats you like a maid? Cheats on you?

Ugh. People do occasionally do terrible things before we realize it. I'm sorry. At least now you know that this particular person can't be trusted with your precious time.

Money gives you the ability to abandon an unhealthy relationship quickly. Wiggle rooms means you can summon the necessary resources to exit and move on with your life. I promise you that you'll find it a lot easier to leave if you have some cash and a way to sustain yourself. Money gives you the freedom to let go of the wrong person. It grants you independence.

Even Judge Judy herself knows this truth. She recounted this conversation with her first husband in one of her books:*[2]

> *I said to Ron, who was in private practice and could set his own hours, "I have to be in court tomorrow afternoon. You need to go to the swim meet." He had a look of incredulity. "That's not our deal. If you want to work, that's fine, but your job is a hobby." [...]*
> *We were divorced within a year, and I vowed to never again let another person define me.*

Now she is worth hundreds of millions of dollars and gets to yell at people for a living. What a life.

If the unhealthy relationship is at work, wiggle room means being able to storm out triumphantly. Your boss exists only to swear at you? Oh, crap; she's flirting with you and making you uncomfortable? He's asking you to do something illegal or unethical?

I'm sorry that you've run into an unhappy situation in the world. It happens.

Having wiggle room lets you put yourself first and wiggle out. If you have your own money to back up your

---

* I want to have lunch with Judge Judy, but I'm afraid I'd just stare at her with my mouth agape the entire time. I heart you, Judy. Not in a creepy way.

reactions, you'll find it a lot easier to leave and find a new job or complain to human resources or even blow the whistle without obsessing over the repercussions.

You'll also have a lot more clout with work if you're prepared to walk away. Even if you love your job, surely there are parts you don't. With financial security, you can ask for accommodations and do your job on your own terms. Maybe work from home on Fridays or commander your own office or come to work in sweatpants. Wiggle room gives you leverage. The more wiggle you have, the more leverage you have.

Wiggle room also means being able to extricate yourself from a negative living situation. I see so many unhappy living arrangements on *Judge Judy* that could easily be solved with a healthy balance in a bank account.

The crazy and violent roommate is someone you just don't get along with? The place doesn't have functioning heat? Whoops, the house you rented on Craigslist is actually an empty parking lot? That really sucks.

As Judy likes to shout, "Move!" If it's that bad, just move. Money lets you follow that very sound advice. Cash as servant will help you pack.

Wiggle room also means the ability to navigate the justice system if necessary. Even Judy doesn't get it right all the time. I mean, I've never seen her get it wrong, but she's helped dole out justice for more than forty-five years. I assume she's made a mistake at least once when doling. If you're on the other side of the mistake, having an *Avoid-Judy's-Wrath Fund* lets you shrug off the verdict. It's basically small claims, so nothing to ruin your life over.

Even more importantly, if your brush with the law is something bigger, money obviously helps. Caught smoking a joint in public? Arrested for protesting something you found abhorrent? Even for misdemeanors, you better have bail money or else you'll sit in a cell until it's all sorted.

Overworked public defenders with crushing caseloads simply cannot give you the same defense that a gaggle of attorneys working solely for you can. Money talks. It's a sad reality that the justice system can peek under her blindfold or at least put her pinky on the scale if you wave enough cash in her face. Sometimes.

Wiggle room means taking ownership of your existence and taking care of yourself. Tell John Cash, first and foremost, to sew up your parachute, umbrella, and safety net. Ask him to whisper in your ear that you'll be fine, even without the system's official support. Knowing that you'll be okay when the universe accidentally hurls lemons at you changes everything.

Unfortunate things will still happen to you. That's a given. Anticipate it. Life is a game of chance and occasionally it will deal you out a terrible hand. It is so much more fun to play with these hands if you have a little bit of cushion. Plans are worthless, but planning is everything. That's wiggle room.

I'm not saying everything will be easy, but I can guarantee that everything will be *harder* with no money in the bank. When Lady Luck pushes you away— something that I promise you with 100% certainty will happen from time to time—you can breathe deeply and console your financial avatar. This is why you have money.

Spend money on what you repeatedly do

After you buy the necessities, you can buy control over your life. Control your time. Do you have autonomy? Are you doing what you want to do?

Here's how you can find contentment on a day-to-day basis: find something that you like to do and then do that thing repeatedly. If you think you're constantly getting better at that thing and that you're making a difference in the world with that thing, then you've pretty much won the game of life. You've turned your passion into your purpose.

For me, finding something I wanted to do was the hardest part. What's the best way to leave a legacy? Raising young people? Curing cancer? Convincing people you're right? Saving the llamas? Sleeping? Chasing mindless hedonism?

If that's the hardest part for you too, autonomy means you can carve out as much time, energy, and mental space as possible to finding that thing you want to be repeatedly doing. That's the route I took. I built up my savings in a job that filled my days but didn't thrill my soul. After I had my version of enough, *then* I went looking for my thing.

That's not the only way to be happy with money, of course. Some people stumble across their thing early. They grittily and eagerly follow that thing. Through their grit and eagerness, they inevitably find success. Their passion assures them they have enough money to be happy. They love their work because it's not a job to them. It's not even a career. It's a calling. A purpose.

Lucky jerks.

If you enjoy the thing you're repeatedly doing and that thing makes you money, well, isn't that the dream? Your passion making you money? Getting out of bed each day impatient to tackle that day's challenge, solving it regularly, while simultaneous making money and your mark on the world. Can you imagine? Some people have that. Why can't I? Why can't you?

You are what you repeatedly do. If you can happily do something that makes you money for the rest of your life, then it doesn't matter how long your working life is. My babbling is entertaining, but maybe not useful for you. You were the first to fist bump me.

Enjoyment of time is primary. Money is secondary. That's *Operation Enough!* You have complete control. What do you want the story of your life to look like? Money gives you the freedom to decide. You have only so much energy for a given day. If your day job you hate takes up all your energy, you don't have anything left to give to the rest of your world. When you free up your time, your brain can concentrate on designing your life. You have time to cultivate who you are.

After you've bought your time and you've figured out your thing, you get to do your thing repeatedly. Congratulations. You now have the time to perfect your chosen craft. Get better at it. Keep learning and creating and doing with respect to your thing. That's what makes people happy. If you do that, you're pretty much guaranteed to be successful in life because you're living the life you're meant to live.

And even if you have no idea what your passion is supposed to be, that's okay, too. I know that's pretty heavy.

It's still pretty marvelous having control over your time. With enough, you can tailor your energy level to match your activity. This change can improve your life an astonishing amount if your body clock doesn't align with your current work schedule. Personally, I'm a night owl and dislike getting up early. I sleep when I'm tired and wake up when I'm not. This might be my favorite thing about my life.

You can play with your schedule to see what works for you. Exercise in the morning? Or the evening? When are you hungry? Enough lets you listen to your body. What is ideal for you personally? It might not be what you think.

Having control over your time also lets you do things *when* most people aren't doing them. I'm pretty sure it's much easier to get a tee time for golf at 11 a.m. on a Wednesday rather than on a Saturday.

Oh yeah, spend on your hobbies. Especially if you don't know your purpose. Hobbies are a good way to pass the time. That's a good reason to get out of bed. That's something to look forward to.

Having a couple of real hobbies makes you an interesting person. An authentic person. Hobbies: good. But the hobby must be real to justify summoning John Cash. This is where the know yourself part comes into play.

So, what's your real hobby? If you know and you've thought about the purchase and you believe it will make your hobby more enjoyable, I won't complain. That's how you *should* spend money.

If you're a biker and you want to buy a fancy pair of gloves to keep your hands warm, I say more power to you, my good man! You bowl in a league regularly and you want to buy a fancy pair of gloves to grip the ball smartly? I'm not surprised that's a thing. You're all about fashion and found a fancy pair of gloves that go perfectly with your coat? You can't tell because this isn't a real conversation, but I'm shrugging my indifference.

Just be thoughtful about it.

If you crochet, do you need to buy another needle? I know you love baseball, but is purchasing a T-shirt at every game necessary? Yeah, video games are your hobby, but can you play more with the games you already have?

Seriously, I'm asking.

I don't know your answers because I don't know you, but if you do and if those things bring you joy, hobby away! Only you know what's important enough to spend your money on. You would probably consider the amount I spend on my travel hobby excessive. Or at least abnormal.

So, to recap, spend your money on what you do every day. If you don't like the thing you do every day, spend your money buying your time so you can figure out what you want to do every day. When you know what you want to do every day, do it and happily spend money on doing it.

Buy the ability to say yes to adventure and friendship

Another big piece of the happiness puzzle is cultivating healthy relationships. It's all meaningless unless you have people to do it all for and with.

My version of enough also means having enough money to nurture relationships and say yes to adventure and possibility. And—pro tip—after you buy your time, you find oodles of opportunities to say yes.

Think about your pals for a minute. Which friend are you closer with? The one who can never do anything because they're always broke? Or the one who is always saying yes to your suggestions of hanging out?

Be the type of person who says yes. At least be the type of person who *can* say yes. Good family and friends are a major component of happiness. I suppose you could add good coworkers to that list, but since I don't have a job, I won't.

We're social creatures and we crave social bonds. If your day-to-day interactions with other people aren't stressful, but rather fun and comforting, your life will be better. It sounds so obvious. A happy, healthy, and supportive environment nurtures happy, healthy, and supportive people.

My lucky spot in the universe included the best family in existence. I know everyone can't say that. I read about an entire generation in China who have no brothers and no sisters; whose children will have no cousins, no aunts, and no uncles. What a lonely thought.

If you don't have a great family, that stinks. I'm sorry. The good news is that you can surround yourself with good friends. Are you interacting with the people you want to be interacting with? Hanging out and doing things that are fun and that interest you with other people who are fun and interesting makes you fun and interesting. Honest!

When I said spend money on relationships, I don't mean bribing people to hang out with you. I mean going out and doing things with people whose company you enjoy. Choose experiences over stuff. Go have dinner. Or drinks. Experience life. Make memories. That's what I do. Spend money on creating possibility. Concert for a band you've never heard of? An art class? Roller skating? Cook and then eat dinner? Go do stuff. Don't go buy stuff. Buy your autonomy so you can do stuff with people.

How to make friends
Knowing how to make friends has done heaps for my happiness level. Heaps. I don't know how to quantify it. I can give you a bit of advice about it, though. In April 2015, I started a project I called, *Operation Enjoy the Crap Out of Sydney While I Still Can*. This was my attempt to make the most out of my last six months living in Australia. This not-at-all classified operation entailed me making plans to do something Every. Single. Day. The rules are simple.

***Operation Enjoy* rules**
1. Plan something fun to do every day.
2. The "something" must be outside your home if you're by yourself.

This operation is how I discovered the secret to making friends. Instead of just waiting and saying yes when people ask you to do things with them, you do the asking.

Okay, so maybe this advice is obvious for the rest of humanity who seem to know exactly what they're doing on this giant rock hurtling through space, but this realization changed my world.

Prior to starting *Operation Enjoy*, and after living in Sydney for more than a year, I had three close friends that I spoke to regularly and another half-dozen acquaintances that I spoke to sporadically. By the time I left Sydney six months later, I had a dozen close friends that I spoke to regularly and another dozen acquaintances.

This transition was not easy for me because, at my core, I fear I am a socially awkward, shy, introverted, reclusive hobbit.

Don't get me wrong, I'm friendly. I can make friends when the making is easy and convenient. I cherish the close friends I had in my insulated middle and high school. The dozens of booze-filled networking events in law school made making friends comically simple.

But in the "real world" outside of school and as an adult working a job that demanded too many of my hours, I found making friends extremely difficult. Post-law school in Chicago, I tended to socialize with family who lived close by.

When I moved to Sydney, though, I did not know a soul, and while that thought delighted my misanthropic tendencies, it terrified the much larger part of me that despised my misanthropic tendencies.

When I feel nervous, I tend to put on my lawyer trousers and research my way out of the anxiety. Apparently, there are three conditions that are crucial to making close friends:[3]

1. Proximity
2. Repeated, unplanned interactions
3. A setting that encourages people to let their guard down and confide in each other

The first condition was easy enough to conquer. Sydney boasted more than four million humans in "close proximity" to me. Surely, I could tolerate and eventually even like a handful of them.

The third condition was also fairly simple. Like much of the world, Australia's culture relies heavily on the imbibing of alcohol. If that's not a setting that encourages people to let their guard down and confide in each other, I don't know what is.

The second condition was the one that confused me. The repeated interactions part I understand because the number of interactions I have with someone determines which box in my brain—friend, acquaintance, or stranger danger—they should crawl into. The "unplanned" bit, though, had me stymied. Real life isn't like television. People don't just drop by unannounced.

Okay, so it's one thing to understand empirically how to make friends (which I still didn't), and it's another to put it into actual practice. This is why I liked *Operation Enjoy* so much. Per my own rules, I *had* to do something every single day. I exhausted my "close friends" pool fairly early on so I reached out to acquaintances more often. Eventually, my acquaintances turned into friends.

On the inevitable day when nobody I knew could accompany me, I ventured out alone and struck up conversations with strangers. I would exchange contact information with people I found interesting and invite them to do things with me later.

That's the scary part, but also the exhilarating part. And, like most things in life, it gets easier the more you do it.

The logistics of *Operation Enjoy* involved a lot of lists. I would print out a weekly calendar and a monthly calendar, look at my various lists—my Australia Bucket list, my *Operation Enjoy* Activity Ideas list, my Monthly To-Do list, my Restaurants People Have Told Me I Should Try list—and slot in activities. I would then invite people to do those things with me.

As soon as I scored a new potential friend and phone number, I would whip out my calendar, figure out which day I had nothing planned and send a text asking my new acquaintance if that day worked for getting together.

As an added bonus, on the occasional days when my plans fell through, staying in felt like an indulgence and not like I was a loser with no social life.

And guess what? I finally understood that part of the research that stymied me years earlier, the "repeated, unplanned interactions" bit. That's the difference between a friend and a close friend. The ones who text you to get together impromptu. The more I asked people to hang out with me, the more people asked me to hang out with them. Eventually my closest friends would text to get together spontaneously.

That's another thing to remember. Say yes when people ask you to do things with them. Go out and do things with other people. Spend money on that. Even if you're an introvert. I bet it'll make your life better.

Operation Enjoy deepened every friendship I had made up to that point. I'm still amazed by how big a difference that made to the quality of my life. I was busy and constantly had something to look forward to. My journal entries were perkier and more interesting. I felt like Sydney was home. I felt like I had a lot of close friends because I had a lot of close friends. I felt…happy.

It's easy to create friendships spending on adventures. It's hard to create friendships spending on stuff. Believe me, nobody is going to come over to look at your toaster oven more than once.

When you share an experience, you are much more likely to encounter a situation where the people who are partaking in the experience with you will let their guard down and confide in you. You can then let your guard down and confide in them. That's how you become friends!

Remember how it's all relative? Each experience you have is unique to you and harder to compare to your neighbors'. Cash as master sells you envy. Cash as servant buys you contentment.

Your experiences make up your memories, which in turn make up you. You're defined by the sum of your experiences and not the shit you've bought along the way.

Here's a specific step-by-step guide that worked for me during *Operation Enjoy* that might work for you. I really like meetup.com, a website that coordinates groups of people with the same interest. A meetup group for every interest. There are even meetup groups for financial independence. I personally like the book clubs and the walking meetups.

How to make friends through meetup.com
1. Go to meetup.com and find some groups in your area within an appropriate radius of where you exist.
2. Pick a group that sounds interesting to you.
3. Attend a meeting.

4. Attend another meeting.
5. Maybe one more.
6. When you've discovered people you enjoy interacting with, swap information.
7. Invite them to do things with you.
8. Do things with them.
9. Be friends.
10. Keep going to the meetup too. You'll meet more people.
11. Repeat steps six through eight.
12. Make more friends.
13. Ask the people you feel most comfortable with to do things with you spontaneously.
14. Have close friends.
15. Enjoy life.

I can make that list much longer, but I feel that way about most of my lists. For instance, if you don't enjoy step three, go back and make sure you've judged step two correctly and the event is something that actually interests you and not just something you think should interest you or you wish would interest you.

Step six could theoretically happen after step three or step four. With some people you will click right away. With most people however, I've found you will need a couple of interactions.

During step eight, let your guard down and confide in these new potential friends. That gets you to step nine.

It takes time and effort and resources to figure out what activities interest you; seek them out, do them, find people who you tolerate, hang out with them, reveal your confidences, and then repeat the whole process. I find it to be mostly worth that time and effort, though. Good friendships are a key component of happiness.

What's really fun is combining a few of the elements of buying happiness. You can buy an experience related to your hobby with friends that do that hobby and refuse to buy crap while doing so.

Are you an athlete? Spend money on the gym and leagues, but not fancy athletic clothes. Cubs fan? Spend money on tickets to the game or a six-pack of beer to entice your friend's company, but not the memorabilia. If you're a traveler, spend money on the activities and not the trinkets.

Super fun!

ACTION PLAN!
HOW DO YOU USE MONEY'S SUPERPOWERS CURRENTLY?

Step 1—Understand your fixed expenses. Write down all your current fixed expenses. These expenses are expenses you can expect to pay on a regular basis. Some fixed expenses vary in amount each month. For these expenses, calculate the average by checking out the last six months or so of your payments.

Fixed expenses include (a non-exhaustive list):
- Rent
- Mortgage
- Property taxes
- Electricity
- Gas
- Internet
- Cable
- Cell phone
- Car payment
- Car insurance

> Health insurance
> Long term disability insurance
> Short term disability insurance
> Renter's insurance
> Home insurance
> Life insurance
> Any other type of insurance
> Minimum debt repayment

Step 2—Understand your income. Figure out your monthly income. How much money do you earn from your job each month? If this amount varies each month, calculate the average from the last six months.

Step 3—What's left? Calculate how much you have left over for your variable expenses each month. Take your average monthly income you calculated in step 2 and subtract your average monthly fixed expenses from step 1.

> **Average monthly income – total average monthly fixed expenses = wiggle room.**

Step 4—How are you spending your wiggle room? Peruse your receipts and credit card and debit card. Look at your spending and ponder the happiness each purchase bought you.

Step 5—Pick the low hanging fruit. Eliminate or cut back on anything obvious that doesn't give you the correct bang for the happiness buck.

CHAPTER 3

How Do I Save?

Enough is your destination, but how do you get there? What time can I expect you? Are there any fun pit stops along the way?

Where are you?
I can't give you directions until you tell me where you are.

If this is the first time you're thinking about this stuff, your financial avatar is a newborn. Cute, but helpless.

The easiest way to diagnose your financial avatar and guesstimate how long it will take you to retire is by figuring out how much of your work income you're saving.

If your savings rate is negative and you have credit card debt, my heart hurts for you. You'll never retire if it's zero and you spend everything you make. If it's, say, 10%, you're "normal," but in for a long working life. My percentage averaged 75% or more when I worked as a lawyer. That's why I was on the short track to retirement.

Increase your income, reduce your expenses, and maximize your savings percentage. That's how you retire early.

So where are you? Do you owe anybody money for anything?

Debt is bad. I'm anti-debt. Vehemently anti-debt. When you tell me you have debt, my mind immediately goes into terror mode. I don't care about great interest rates. A 0% loan from anybody is still a bit of an emergency. Psychologically, being able to say you are debt-free is everything. Not owing anybody anything frees up a lot of brain cells.

In my financial avatar's world, if you owe money, your avatar is a baby. Debt means you have to devote every single ounce of your energy into soothing and cooing. Babies need constant attention and you have no control over your life when you're tasked with keeping one alive. Their schedule dictates your schedule, and their schedule is really unreasonable.

If you're at net worth zero—phew!—you can raise that screaming pile of financial avatar baby into an adorable lump of toddler very quickly. Hopefully by the end of this book!

If you have debt because you financed a house or an education, you may be able to convince me it's necessary if you're eloquent and thoughtful with your explanation. I'll still think of it as a draining evil to eliminate as soon as possible. It's really, really nice not owing anybody money.

If you're in credit card debt, I'm going to stop being nice and yell at you for a minute. Paying interest for a depreciating asset ranks as the most revolting, idiotic, ghastly, lurid, no good move you can make to your financial avatar. To put it mildly. Yet this move is so mind-bogglingly common!

Seriously, my mind is boggling right now just thinking about it. That's like asking Superman to do evil. The stupidest way to use Superman yet.

Your money can do so much more for you than line the balance sheets of banks and credit card companies. If you carry a balance on a credit card, you're paying more for *everything*. Everything! What material object is so important that you're willing to pay more than what that thing is worth? Ack, I'm breaking out in hives just thinking about it.

Having debt on your credit card that you can't pay back immediately is a freaking emergency and should be treated as such. Go into serious mode. Refuse to buy a single unnecessary item until it's paid off. Realize that almost everything is an unnecessary item. Pick one loan and kill it. That's your job. Earn money and get rid of it. Focus only on that goal.

You can pick any debt you darn well please. Mathematically, it makes sense to tackle your highest interest rate one first. But I also like the idea of building momentum and starting with the smallest one.

Personally, I went a bit scatter-shot when I paid off my

student loans, paying off the 8.5% loan first, then the 0% loan to my sister, then the next few highest rate ones and then the smallest debt and then the next highest.

Calculate how soon you can get to zero net worth and countdown to that. Make it a game you can win.

ACTION PLAN!
WHERE ARE YOU?

Let's orient yourself on the map. Where are you in terms of net worth?

Step 1—Know your institutions. List every financial account that you have. Here are some non-exhaustive possibilities:

Debt:
Credit card(s)
Department store card(s)
Student loan(s)
Car loan(s)
Payday loan(s)
Loan(s) from family
Line(s) of credit
Mortgage(s)

Assets:
Checking account(s)

Savings account(s)

Investment account(s)

Retirement account(s)

CD(s)

Equity in real property

Crumpled hundreds in your apocalypse bunker

Step 2—Make sure your financial avatar hasn't been kidnapped. Did you miss anything? Has anyone stolen your identity? Go to annualcreditreport.com and download the reports from all three of the credit agencies, TransUnion, Equifax and Experian. Check your accounts against the list you made in Step 1. Update Step 1 if necessary.

Put a reminder in your calendar for four months from now that says, "Check credit—TransUnion." Put a second reminder in your calendar for eight months from now that says, "Check credit—Equifax." Finally, put a third reminder in your calendar for one year from now that says "Check credit—Experian."

In four and in eight months, go to creditkarma.com. It's a free service that will give you your TransUnion and Equifax credit score anytime you want. It's not the full report, but it's enough information to verify that your financial avatar hasn't started doing drugs or dating an undesirable thug.

In a year, go back to annualcreditreport.com and

download your Experian credit report. You can download the other full credit reports from TransUnion and Equifax if you're feeling ambitious.

The federal government mandates the credit agencies provide a free report to you once a year. This schedule allows you to monitor your financial avatar frequently while not paying anything.[*]

Step 3—What's your debt number? Find the latest paperwork for all of your debt you listed in step one and fill in the following information on a spreadsheet.

> Loan name
> Current balance
> Interest rate
> Due date (what day of the month?)
> Minimum payment
> Website name
> Username
>
> **Optional additional categories**
> Order to pay
> Website password
> Amount borrowed initially

---

[*] Personally, I freeze my credit with all three of the credit agencies as well. Freezing your credit gives you one additional layer of security against identity theft—a pin code. You'll have to jump through a few more hoops when applying for credit in the future. The price of the freeze depends on your state. My state mandates a charge of $5 or less.

Step 4—What are your assets? Find the latest paperwork for all your assets you listed in step one and fill in the following information on a spreadsheet.

    Asset name
    Liquid amount
    Non-liquid amount
    Website name

Optional additional category
Website password

Step 5—Calculate your net worth. Simple math! Total assets minus total debts. Some people will want to include the value of their stuff—their cars and furniture and such. You *can*, but I don't like that idea. It's hard to know exactly how much you could get for your things and how long it would take you to sell. I prefer cash to stuff because cash's power is pretty straightforward.

Don't buy stuff

Here's an easy way to tame the money monster. Don't waste money on depreciating assets. Things. Stuff. Crap. Junk. Buying another unnecessary depreciating asset before you have your *Avoid-Judy's-Wrath Fund* is the stupidest decision you can make. Don't do that.

Stuff won't make you happy. Not for long anyway. You adapt to the shiny things surprisingly quickly and constantly need new stuff and more things to replicate the initial happiness buzz. It's a short-term high and never a long-term solution.

Advertising is an entire industry brimming with smart, driven, competent people with a very clear objective: to make you want a certain thing, to insinuate your life isn't complete until you own this thing, and to explain why this new thing is so much better than your old thing. They create an itch and their product is the calamine lotion.[*] They're really good at their jobs. Don't buy crap just because that billboard tells you to. Ignore the billboard!

It's all relative. Your things are easy to compare to other people's things. The newer model is probably nicer than last year's model. It has different features, and it comes in cobalt blue.

The envy lady, Ms. Cash, thrives in this space.

---

[*] Season 1, Episode 13 of the television show *Mad Men* is where I got the calamine lotion information.

Stuff is the shiny things you acquire and want. We all purchase stuff. I purchase stuff. I'm not ashamed.

Junk is the old stuff that you have and no longer want or use. It's the things you throw away or donate or leave in a remote corner of your home that you're no longer able to access because you're a hoarder.

All the stuff that you buy in the store will eventually be relegated to the dumpster. The rate of stuff turning to junk may vary based on the purchase, but eventually, everything will be tossed. Everything. As far as the environment and your financial avatar is concerned, the only difference between stuff and junk is the packaging and the destination.

You'll never get rich spending your money on depreciating assets. I know we live in a culture of easy credit and a constant barrage of advertisements enticing you to buy now and pay later. Why wait? You can find a company to help you finance just about anything. Everyone does it.

Don't be stupid. I already yelled at you about this. Don't turn your money into junk. I'm going to nag you about this for the remainder of the book. Sorry in advance.

How should you shop?

I realize that you do occasionally need to buy stuff. When you do, though, be thoughtful about it. That's all I'm asking. Make sure the stuff you bring into your life is worthy of your money and your attention.

I make a lot of lists, and two of my "staple lists," if you will, are my Needs List and my Wants List. Once every week or so, I sit down and brainstorm. On the first list, the Needs List, I write down everything I need. On the second list, the Wants List, I write down everything I want.

Differentiating between a need and a want is a crucial step in bulking up your financial avatar. Hint: almost everything is a want.

Here's a fictitious example:

Needs
Toilet Paper
Bread
Saline solution

Wants

The latest video game console

A new dress

A trip to Boise

When I went shopping, I would bring only my Needs List and buy only those items. Done and dusted.

For my Wants List, I would analyze the hell out of every Want and ask myself the following questions:

1. Is this an item that I know to be useful or believe to be beautiful?
2. What is the opportunity cost of using that money instead of investing it?
3. Will buying this item make my life better or worse in the long run?
4. What are the externalities of that item?

Let's take a look at each question more closely.

1. Beautiful or useful?

I pilfered this idea from a designer named William Morris. This is his golden rule. "Have nothing in your houses that you do not know to be useful, or believe to be beautiful."[4]

I mostly use this question when I shop for clothes, perhaps once a year.

I'll take just about anything that fits me that my sisters

offer, but if I'm buying a new item, I must love it and I must wear it.

It's probably a dress with pockets that is designed to go without a bra. Those are the best.

2. Opportunity cost?

Economics is my scene, and opportunity cost is a core idea in that discipline. What are you giving up with your choices? Opportunity costs exist in everything. Every single decision you make closes off a million different options. What opportunity did you miss with your decision? How much would you have if you invested that money instead? Every time I make a purchase, I consider the amount of money I'd lose long-term.

I used to get estimates of whatever it was I wanted to buy and consider what Five-Years-from-Now-Anita would choose. I'd then imagine the life cycle of the objects in question.

Here is a fictitious example using that Wants List I made earlier: Do I want that latest video game console for a mere $400?

Anita buys the gaming system

Year 1: Brand new video game console! This is making me happier than joy itself.

Year 2: I bought a few more games. I still play.

Year 3: Meh, it's not the latest model anymore.
Year 4: It's not plugged in.
Year 5: It's gathering a lot of dust. Oh, I should buy the newest console. That'll make me happy!

Anita invests her money wisely (more on that later)
Year 1: I've made a lousy $28 on my investment. Maybe I should have bought that video game console…
Year 2: Huh, now I'm up almost $58.
Year 3: Wow, $90 in interest. With my $400 in principal, that's enough to buy the newer video game console and still have some money left over.
Year 4: $124 in interest!
Year 5: My net worth is $560 higher than if I had bought the video game system. Wowzers.

The opportunity cost for me to buy a video game console today is $561.02 less for Five-Years-from-Now-Anita.

The last video game I could claim any ability in was Super Mario World in the 90s. I'm not a gamer. I would not be tempted with a new video game console.

But I do need clothes occasionally. What if I need a new dress? I have complete control over how much I spend on that dress.

Anita is a fan of the Duchess of Cambridge and buys a copy of the dress Kate wore for her engagement photo, for $700.

Year 1: I wore the dress for two fancy occasions. I got so many compliments. You wouldn't believe.

Year 2: I wore it twice more. It's probably my favorite dress.

Year 3: There are too many pictures of me on Facebook in it.

Year 4: I could probably sell it on eBay for a couple of hundred bucks. It's a famous dress.

Year 5: It sits in my closet looking pretty.

Anita finds a dress at the thrift store for $20. She takes $680 and invests it.

Year 1: I have $727.60. I could buy the Duchess's dress *and* another thrift store dress.

Year 2: I've worn my dress about twelve times already in the past couple of years.

Year 3: $153.03 just in interest!

Year 4: I still wear the dress occasionally.

Year 5: Dress has been donated back to thrift store. $953.74 total for my investment.

The opportunity cost for me to buy the fancy dress now is $953.74 less for Five-Years-from-Now-Anita.

So, I'm not a fashionista, and I wouldn't be tempted

with the dress, either. I do, however, like adding places to my "visited" list. What if I wanted to go to Boise, Idaho?

Anita goes to Boise for $500.
Year 1: Fun trip!
Year 3: "Oh, you are from Boise? I have visited Boise. We shall use this topic to start a conversation at this dinner party."
Year 5: Flipping through pics and remembering how fun that was.

Anita doesn't go to Boise and invests.
Year 1: What the heck is in Boise?
Year 3: $612.52! Woooooooot!
Year 5: $701.28! I'm rich!

The opportunity cost for me to take a $500 trip to Boise now is $701.28 less for Five-Years-from-Now-Anita.

I actually used to calculate how much Forty-Years-from-Now-Anita would have for everything, because the numbers are so much more impressive the further out in time you go.

None of this is to say that you should refuse to buy anything and live in a cardboard box. Pick and choose your Wants depending on what makes you happiest. Know yourself!

Maybe that video game console is worth $400 because you'll be spending hundreds of hours playing with it. If fashion is your hobby, okay, enjoy the dress. Maybe, like me, travel is your passion. I want to go to Boise.

Just understand what you're giving up and realize that the more wants you indulge in, the poorer you will be.

3. Better or worse off in the long run?

Will buying this item make my life better or worse off in the long run? If the answer is clearly worse off in the long run, though, I don't buy it. Everything I spend my powerful dollars on should, at the very least, make my life neutral when I look at the big picture.

I suppose I can also try to convince myself that the outcome is uncertain, that I don't actually know if the net result overall will be positive or negative. At the very least, I must be able to make a compelling argument. That's what it means to be thoughtful. Make a compelling argument.

4. Externalities?

The first three questions force me to consider what buying that particular item would mean to me. The fourth question prods me to consider the costs to people who aren't Anita.

For people who don't think in jargon, my apologies. An externality is an additional cost (or benefit) that is not imposed on the person causing the externality. For example, let's say two cars on the freeway three miles ahead of you crash and cause a traffic jam. As a result of this, you're stuck in traffic limbo and lose an hour's worth of work. Yup, those two cars most definitely caused that additional cost to you. But they won't bear the cost. Because life's unfair sometimes.

Pollution is another example. When people drive, they pay a certain amount at the gas station. That cost includes the cost to extract, refine, and deliver the gasoline to the gas station. It also includes the price of labor, rent, and, of course, profit for everyone involved. There are probably a lot of other costs I'm missing.

The price at the pump almost certainly does not take into account the true adverse cost to the environment and your grandchildren, though. That harm is borne by the entirety of the world and the future through the resulting climate change. Those types of costs are nebulous and uncertain, therefore difficult to calculate and almost never added to the sticker price. As humans, we are quick to reap the benefits, but slow to comprehend the costs.*[5]

After doing this contemplation of costs for a while, I began to realize that almost nothing was worth the actual price. When you think about the costs involved and ditch some habits from your route that don't make you happy, you not only pad your net worth, you're also probably making the world better.

---

* This is a quote from biologist, Barry Commoner. Apropos of nothing, his name would make an excellent spy name.

Operation Buy Everything on Your Wants List, but Evaluate the Purchase Two Months Later to See if It Made Your Life Better helped me realize this truth even more. At the beginning of one month, I went out and bought everything on my Wants List. No thinking. No waiting. No calculating, just shopping. I wasn't going to do any stinking math. Before I did though, I set a calendar reminder to talk to myself about the purchases in two months.

I bought a cat scratcher that my foster cat used exactly zero times. There was the fancy litter box that I'm pretty sure she felt, at best, indifferent toward. Curtains for the extra mini-bedroom and the one-piece swimsuit for my swimming lessons. A new purse and a necklace.

Two months later, I had enjoyed only the swimsuit. Perhaps my two guests enjoyed the curtains for a grand total of three nights. I don't know. I moved a short while later and never used them again.

A lot of items on my Wants List fall off the Wants List after a few weeks and a few thoughts spent sitting on the purchase. Buying everything I wanted helped me tap into that buyer's remorse when I realized how little joy impulsive shopping actually brought me. I conjure that feeling when contemplating future purchases.

Do I really want this thing? Or is this a passing fancy? Today, I still have a Wants List, but it's more of a reminder than anything.

I've internalized all these questions. One of the many reasons I dislike shopping and don't buy much stuff is because I can take nearly any item on my Wants List, calculate the real price with the externalities included and decide it is most certainly not worth what the sticker suggests.

My financial avatar consults my environmental geek and appeals to my humanity and I usually end up not wanting the item in the end. It *really* has to make my life better to warrant the purchase.

Case study: a television

What if you gave up your television?

I know! I know! You're shaking your head at me, irritated with my idiocy. A television is a freaking necessity. I'm losing my credibility for even suggesting going without. I hear you! TV is amazing. I grew up on TV. I used my parents' hand-me-down televisions for the first few years of my adult life without a thought.

But when I moved to Australia, well, the wall sockets were different. I'd have to buy one there. Let me show you a hint of my derangement using two fictitious voices in my head, in the form of Mimi and Ms. Cash as I walk past the following sign:

Samsung! Huge TV! $699.99! You save $100! Free delivery! So many exclamation points!

Ms. Cash: Oh my! It's a sign from the gods. This television is exactly the amount you have in your pocket.

Mimi: $700 is a fair price for the actual television set, but let me consider the true cost with all the additional expenses, opportunity costs, and likely externalities. [*Note: My financial avatar isn't much fun at a party.*]

First, you have to pay taxes. Everyone wants a cut here. The federal government imposes sales taxes on certain items, and depending on where you live, the state, county, and city taxes will increase the price of an item by as much as 10%. I wish the amount advertised included taxes, like it does in other countries.

Ms. Cash: Here it's only 6.25%, or another $43.75. You can still afford that.

Mimi: What about usage costs? Unless you expect me to use the television as a very inappropriate paperweight, I have to pay to use the television.

Ms. Cash: According to the Energy Guide sticker on the side of the television, your energy costs will only go up about $14/year.

Mimi: Well, according to the fine print on the Energy

Guide Sticker, that $14 is calculated assuming eleven cents per kilowatt-hour and television usage of five hours a day. My energy company charges me twenty to twenty-eight cents per kilowatt-hour depending on if I'm using during peak hours. And after all the various fees and taxes, in reality, I'm actually paying closer to twenty-two cents per kilowatt-hour on average. That means my actual energy costs will rise about $28/year.

Ms. Cash: That's still a reasonable amount! Plus, the seller generously offers free delivery! Suckers!

Mimi: Presumably the sellers are normal business people and the cost of transport is built into the price of the television. "Free" delivery is a marketing gimmick. And it's only free delivery as long as I overcome the instant gratification impulse and don't choose the "expedited" or "express" delivery options.

Ms. Cash: Let's get more information from the salesperson.

Salesperson: For an additional $79.95, the television comes with a "protection plan." This means if anything happens to the television in the next two years, you'll get a new TV for free!

Mimi: Well, it's not free. It's another $79.95 right now.

Come on, what are the odds this television is going to break in the next two years? And that "protection plan" (i.e. insurance or extended warranty) contract must be four pages long with loopholes galore. Who buys these? [*Mimi reads the protection plan contract terms, her mouth agape the entire time.*]

The list of reasons the insurance company can use to deny your claim is long and arduous and covers seemingly every possibility from floods to terrorism to scratches to contact with any human or animal bodily fluids. I struggled mightily to come up with an argument to spend this additional $80 and failed miserably.

Salesperson: Okay. It's almost Father's Day. Would you like to include a $50 gift card with your purchase?

This is where I told the voices in my head to shut up. I hate add-ons because I know that I'm susceptible to them. You probably are, too. The research on decision-making and willpower finds that these two qualities are like muscles.[6]

The more willpower you exhibit early on, the less willpower you have for later decisions. The more decisions you have to make in a day means you are increasingly likely to make poor decisions or go with the default option. If you've already said no to the protection plan and the installation fee, you're much more likely to indulge in the expedited or express shipping.

Just say no initially and walk away! Don't tax your willpower.

You're still irritated with me over my suggestion? Okay, that's completely fair. Maybe a television is the best way to spend your hard-earned cash. It might be again for me one day. But here's how I answered the four questions for this Want.

1. Is this an item that I know to be useful or believe to be beautiful?

This is an easy yes. A television would allow me to watch *Judge Judy*, which I do quite enjoy. That would be useful. And the screen is shiny, so that could be beautiful.

Buy, buy, buy!

2. What is the opportunity cost of using that money instead of investing?

If I bought only the television and resisted all the add-ons, the television would cost $743.75 in year 0 and $28 in energy usage every year after. If instead I took that money and put it in a fund earning 7% per year, in forty years, I would have more than $17,000. I'll tell you about this fund in a later chapter.

This number is actually much higher because it's based on the unlikely assumption that I'll never upgrade the television and that the initial purchase lasts forty years. I also assume that

I don't succumb to the temptation of getting cable or a satellite dish and stick with free local TV. Yeah, right.

An extra $17,000 in my sixties isn't enough of an incentive to forgo buying something that is kind of a necessity.

Buy, buy, buy!

3. What are the externalities of that item?

Let me say first that this question about externalities is all well and good and important to consider, but the exact same answers I'm about to give could be given about the laptop I'm currently typing on or the Kindle on the table next to me. This question is more to remind myself to consume less and make sure that the Want is really worth it.

a. What are the environmental implications for the production and distribution of this product?

Producing a television is a complicated industrial process. From the mining of resources for various parts, to the packaging to the fossil fuels used in all the vehicles during the process, our planet recoils.

Every single component in a television requires gutting the earth and polluting the skies and waters and making the future less hospitable.

I know. A bit of a bummer.

b. What were the conditions for the person making this item?

At least one part of that television, more likely than not, will be made by someone in a factory working interminably long hours in horrific conditions for an astonishingly small percentage of the $743.75 I fork over.

c. What will happen to that item once it is no longer useful or beautiful?

Televisions lose their technological "edge" pretty quickly. I doubt many people will use the same television for the next forty years and the odds are good the television will end up in a landfill.

d. Does buying this item help someone else greatly?

Externalities can be positive, too. There have to be some winners somewhere. Remember that car crash from earlier that delayed your arrival to work? If, instead of going to work, you were on your way to the party of a friend who you secretly hate, you'd be happy for the delay. That's a positive externality.

Buying the television may help the economy in the short run, boosting the bottom line of shareholders in Samsung and the box store I buy it from and ensuring that the workers who manufactured, assembled, and sold it will have a job for one more day. You could argue that poor pay in a factory is better than no pay doing nothing.

Consumerism is usually inherently destructive, but…television is a necessity, right? At least as necessary as your cell phone.

Buy, buy, buy. But I'm saying it now without exclamation points.

4. Will buying this item make my life better or worse in the long run?

This question is the one with the most bullshit. You can argue that anything will make your life better in the long run if you want it enough. Just make a good case for yourself. Be honest and thoughtful. Try to argue both sides.

A television might make my life better. I think flipping on the old boob tube is a nice and relaxing way to end the day, to shut your brain off before going to bed. I could potentially be less stressed. I could save money on entertainment.

Sadly, I tend towards laziness and can spend an embarrassing number of hours a day staring at that box. Entire weekends and evenings can vanish, binging on that entertaining and addictive box.

Without a television, I'm so much more productive and social. I also like myself better and feel healthier when

I'm not a couch potato. Finally, I don't see as many commercials and advertisements, which means my brain doesn't ferment as many new Wants.

Mimi wins and I walk away.

Your answers to these questions may be different. And that's okay.

This question about the long run tended to sway my decisions for most of my purchases. What did I want for myself in the big picture? That stuff? Or the possibility of a bigger life?

I pick on stuff, things, consumer goods, junk as a personal finance geek because I know that much of a person's budget (and debt) comes from these items and because these expenses are usually not recurring, necessary, or fixed and thus easier to cut. The average American easily owns more consumer goods than anyone in any society in the history of the world[7] so most people can find items to eliminate. Spending your money on depreciating assets will never make you rich, and most depreciating assets give you the least bang for your happiness buck.

The brilliance of my strategy is that I don't think about money at all. I buy whatever I want, whenever I want. The key is: I just don't want that much. When you weigh the pros and cons of most every purchase, you'll realize eventually that you don't want that much either.

Theoretically.

Buy used

I know that occasionally you still need (or more likely just want) some stuff to live your life. If you take advantage of the cavalier attitude most people have toward consumption, you can strengthen your financial avatar and help the environment at the same time. Buy used goods.

We live in an incredibly and, dare I say, shamefully wasteful society. Consumerism and constantly buying new crap is how we measure the growth of our economy. We throw away instead of fixing what's broken. Upgrading to the newest electronic gadget the day it's available is normal and expected. We are always trying to keep up with the Joneses.

Screw the Joneses. You don't even like the Joneses. You'll never get rich spending your money on depreciating assets. Peruse Craigslist.org, Gumtree.com, garage sales, thrift stores, the Salvation Army. All of these places are overflowing with the various accouterments of your life at prices that would surprise you.

I didn't buy a television when I moved to Australia, but I did buy other things. I bought a washing machine, a microwave, an iron, a flat iron for straightening my hair, a blender, a heater, a fan, a modem, a vacuum, a double bed for the guest room, a blanket, an electric blanket, four pillows and sheets, extra sheets for the bed (brand new and still in the bag!), mesh bags, wine glasses, a stepping stool, and a bike.

As you know, I like making lists, and after consulting my "Crap I Bought for Sydney" list, I know exactly how much I paid for all of this stuff. I bought everything used off Gumtree except for the flat iron, the electric blanket, and the blender. Excluding those three items, I paid a grand total of $330 Australian Dollars for it all.

I didn't buy my items all at once, but rather over the course of a couple of months. That delay requires some patience, but you have patience. I did look in real stores out of curiosity. If I could not delay my gratification and instead bought everything new, I would have shelled out more than $1,300 AUD.

When I left Sydney almost two years later, I threw myself a going-away party which I dubbed *Operation Get Rid of My Booze Because the United States Has Really High Duty Taxes on Alcohol* and made every item listed above available to friends for free. Whatever was left over, I sold on Gumtree. Taking my profit from the sold items into account, I spent only $190, but I am confident I could have recouped the entire $330 were it not for my incredibly generous (and modest) soul.

Anyway, the moral of my story is to buy used, my darlings. Not only did I save a substantial sum of money, I also felt like I was helping the environment by rescuing these items from an early landfill grave. And I prevented the making, packaging, and transportation of new products, guarding Mama Earth once again.

Oh, and a caveat. I had a list drawn up of things that I knew would make my life better. I don't hunt through these sites for random good deals when I don't need anything specific.

Some people can make a pretty penny reselling items they find second-hand, but I am not one of those people. If you are not one of those people either, I do not recommend scanning sites just for the sake of scratching your shopping itch. Buy only what you need and not because you find something cheap.

When you do buy stuff, take care of it! Don't leave it out in the rain or throw it really hard trying to get it on the top shelf of your closet. If it's in good shape, you can use it longer, and when you no longer want to use it, you can sell it. You'll fetch a higher price if it looks pretty and still works well.

Use the heck out of your stuff. Try to fix it if it's broken and don't just automatically toss it and purchase a new one. Honestly, it's super-satisfying fixing something tangible with your hands.

Waste not, want not.

Sell what you don't need

A great way to kick off your financial journey is to go through your house and decide what brings you joy and what doesn't. If you're well into your financial journey, it can still be a fun pit stop along the way. Clear your clutter.

If you find things that are taking up unnecessary space and energy, you can sell them. Put that money toward that debt you picked to kill off. Or to your retirement plan. Ferreting through your junk and deciding what to give up is one of life's joys. It's so freeing!

Stuff exists to make you happy and everything you own desperately wants to be used. When you have too much stuff, you suffer and the stuff suffers because it's not fulfilling its purpose. Sad. It's better to send the stuff you don't need any more off to its next adventure rather than hold it prisoner.

I recommend reading *The Life-Changing Magic of Tidying Up* by Marie Kondo and following her method for discarding your stuff. She articulates exactly what should remain in your house and how you make those decisions. Handle each item in your house and decide if it brings you joy. If it does, that's awesome. Keep it!

I'm not telling you to get rid of everything you own and live in the tall grass down by the river. I'm telling you to be thoughtful about the stuff you let into your home and your life and make sure it brings you enough joy to warrant money's superpowers.

Needing something and then having the item that fulfills that need on hand and easily available is quite satisfying. As soon as you clear out the excess, you'll be able to appreciate the good stuff more.

I'm a minimalist and sold most of my stuff when I left Australia to travel, but my parents aren't. After much cajoling, they agreed to let me and my sister clean out their basement. It's the birthplace of generations of spiders and my hatred of junk. Mom used to work in retail and couldn't resist a deal. Dad thinks every piece of paper deserves consideration. After more than twenty-five years of neglect, the bottom floor of my parent's pad screamed out for attention.

I called this *Operation Clean Out Mom and Dad's Basement and Hold a Garage Sale, Trying to Make Enough Money for a New Couch for Their Living Room.*

We worked for two weeks straight, each devoting eight to twelve hours of our day to clearing, cleaning, and cursing. We also hauled, sorted, and organized. We went through everything in the basement, and everything that didn't spark joy went into one of four categories.

1. Sell
2. Thoughtfully donate
3. Responsibly recycle

4. Throw into the garbage because it has no more useful life left

Category 1—Sell

Anything that you have that is in good condition and that you think someone might pay for, you should try to sell. Use online sites or throw a garage sale. Or both.

We put some of the bigger items on Craigslist—such as a broken fridge.

> Fridge: Nine-year-old GE stainless-steel fridge. We had a repairman come out, and he said it needed a new compressor. If you know anything about fridges and care to fix this beauty, I'm very impressed with your mechanical abilities.

And someone came out and bought it! Instead of having to pay $15 to haul it away, we made $40 by selling it to someone and gave it a second lease on life. Excellent.

You can also widen your reach and sell on a site like eBay. If you're good at that sort of thing, your pool of buyers is much larger than your average garage sale or local website listing. We did try to sell my sister's old wedding dress on eBay, but our three-day auction was unsuccessful. This method of sales requires a type of patience I do not possess. Maybe you do, though.

It's impossible to predict what will be valuable in the future. It's better not to keep stuff just because you hope it will appreciate in value. My mom had collectible Barbie dolls she bought back in the 90s that have been chilling in the basement gathering dust. She paid $40 each for two of them a couple of decades ago, and we resold both for $20. If we had tried the eBay thing with them, we might have gotten $25 each. Maybe.

Collectibles are mostly junk. They're meant to be unopened, so there are a million of them for sale out there that are in brilliant condition. You won't receive a return on this "investment." Old shit has resale value because another person in the world decides it has value and is willing to pay you for it. You can't guess what will be valuable and what will be worthless.

We did have a couple of water guns—unopened, vintage Super Soakers—that we found in the basement. Eventually, my sister sold them on eBay, netting $100. Shipping ate up a lot of the "profit." Shipping and apathy.

You probably have various scraps of metal lying around in your basement and garage. If you take these to a scrap metal recycling place, you can get money for it. We made $4.28 from various scraps of metal we found in the basement.

And, of course, we had a garage sale, selling what we could. In total, we made $665, and I attempted to twerk in celebration. It wasn't enough for a new couch, but it was halfway to a new couch. Plus, the basement now felt happy and fresh.

Holding a garage sale showed me different ways people make themselves happy through shopping. Most people bargained and haggled and triumphed. I get that high. Scoring a great deal can be thrilling. A few people, however, got their thrills from giving us *more* money than the price tag. They understood that, in the end, we were trying to make some cash and since they valued the item they bought more than the sticker price, they had no problem giving us a little extra. They felt good about themselves for their generosity, and, since it's a garage sale, that generosity could be as low as a single dollar. A cheap way to feel good about yourself, eh? This is how you should spend money.

Category 2—Thoughtfully donate

Sometimes it's easier to get rid of your stuff if you can visualize its new life. If you can think of someone who would happily use it and give it to them, everyone wins. You feel good about yourself for donating it. The stuff is happy because it's still useful. The recipient of your gift has a new thing to use for free. Here's what we donated from the basement cleanup:

CDs

Do you remember compact discs? They were big in the 90s as a way to listen to music. If you have any, do you ever actually listen to them anymore? No? You can sell them to a CD store if you know where one exists. We took about forty CDs to a CD store and Mr. CD store owner gave us a whopping $3 for the six discs he deemed worthy. We left the rest behind as a donation to the store. He said they'd at least use the plastic cases again. Win/win.

Books
If your bookshelves are full to overflowing, purge them. We donated books to my favorite place—the library.

Old sheets, blankets, pillows, copy paper, and folders
How much extra bedding do you need? What about office supplies? The animal shelter near my parent's place took these items to use for the animals. Except for the copy paper and folders. I imagine they used that for their business.

Everything left over from the garage sale
We took many trips to Goodwill and the Salvation Army.

Oh, the Goodwill guy may flirt with you.

Category 3—Responsibly recycle

If you find stuff that you can't sell or donate and you don't want to keep, first try investigating how to return it to

Mama Earth as gently as possible. We literally just Googled *[item to recycle] + [city]*. Really easy.

Paper

Paper yellows. Paper molds. Paper rots. Paper stinks. Paper is a fire hazard. Paper invites bugs. Don't be a paper hoarder. Throw out your junk mail as you get it. Or better yet, recycle it!

We dropped off a whopping thirty giant boxes of newspapers, coupons, cardboard, old textbooks, and older magazines to a paper recycling place. This took six trips over two weeks in my parents' van.

Oh, the paper shredder guy may ask you out.

Chemicals

If you've lived in your house for a while, chances are that you probably have a lot of old and random chemicals that you're not allowed to throw into the normal garbage because you care about the environment. Your city probably has a location to deal with these items. We took two trips to a chemical recycling place to drop off old light bulbs and tar and such we found in the basement. There was a giant sign that warned us not to get out of the car, so we just drove up and let the good people working there empty our heavy chemicals while we sat in the air conditioning. I could get used to this.

Paint

Hopefully you can drop off your old paint at the chemical recycling place, but the location near my parents' house didn't accept paint anymore due to budget constraints. Their website offers suggestions like "paint something else!"

We eventually put all the buckets of paint outside with a giant "FREE" sign during the garage sale and got rid of about half of it that way. The rest we let dry out in the hot sun for a few days and threw in with the garbage per the helpful website's less perky suggestion.

Electronics

Remember boomboxes? Or channel-changers? I'm sure you have old stereos and computer parts and such lying around. At one time all of these things were cutting edge and you had to pay a pretty penny for them. Now, you can't give them away. We dropped off old electronics at an electronics recycling place. If you're talented, you may be able to strip the valuable parts inside your electronics and sell them to a scrap metal place.

TVs

Nobody wants your old boxy television. They want the newest, flattest, highest definition television in the store. Once your television is obsolete, it's junk. The electronics recycling place near my parents' place didn't accept old TVs, and they directed us to a parking lot of a gas station that had a giant dumpster somberly moonlighting as a television graveyard. I'm not sure this is a responsible way to recycle it, but there weren't any other options.

Category 4—Throw away
Some things have no useful life left. Nobody wants them, even if you offered them for free. There's no recycling for them. They are destined to lie miserably in a landfill packed tight with other garbage. I worry about our planet. Next time you buy something, imagine where every bit of that purchase is going to end up in fifteen years. Gah, I hate stuff.

What makes your financial avatar smile?
The basic ideas are obvious common sense, right? Spend less than you earn. Maximize your savings percentage. Invest smartly.

God is in the details. What tactics work for you personally and specifically?

Just as our versions of enough are different, the things that work for our financial avatars are also going to be different. And as your financial avatar ages and you bob and weave in between life stages, you'll also need to switch it up.

When I was paying down my student loans and Mimi was a colicky baby, I meticulously listed all my fixed expenses—rent, utilities, minimum student loan payments—in a notebook. For my variable expenses, I just threw everything on my credit card and paid it off in full each month, never carrying a balance. I utilized a Wants List strategy and found I really wanted very little after analyzing the desire.

While working towards financial independence, I simplified even more and stopped splitting my fixed expenses into categories. I just calculated my overall total expenses and my net worth, plotting them on my chart. I bought whatever I wanted, but all my stupid operations gave me a better grasp of what brought me joy.

Court your financial avatar. Be friends. Mimi and I are besties now, but that's only because I took the time to figure out what delights her and what bores her. She doesn't like to micromanage, but she does demand entertainment. She's more of a big picture avatar and doesn't like to get mired down in the details. I hate to say this, but she's also super lazy and can't be bothered a lot.

I know that some people can benefit from tracking how they spend every penny, but I could never get myself to do it. I have no idea how much I spend on any single category.

But maybe you like that structure. There are as many ways to manage your money and save and invest as there are people in a large apartment building. You have to figure what works for you. The good news is you can make it into a game. Because everything can be turned into a game.

I make up new operations testing the various money ideas I stumble across. They usually last a month, but can go for years if Mimi likes the game. You can do anything for a month, and you learn about yourself by going outside your routine and your comfort zone.

Try these month-long operations for yourself to get a better handle on managing your money. Or better yet, make up your own operation and tell me about it. Oh, right; we don't know each other.

Operation Use Only Cash for Everything Except for Rent and Utilities, of Course

Using only cash is a way to track your spending and make you aware. It forces you to evaluate your limited resources and distinguish between a need and a want.

Put a predetermined amount of cash in different envelopes or jars labeled with different budget categories. Food. Entertainment. Kids. You get the idea. Hide the plastic and use only paper.

The point is to learn to spend less than you earn.

List of reasons using only cash might work for you

1. You can spend only what you have in your pocket, so it is literally impossible to spend cash you haven't yet earned.
2. It makes buying expensive junk harder.
3. It forces you to think critically about the Needs List and Wants List.
4. If it gets stolen, you don't have to spend time telling your credit card company. I mean, you *can* spend time telling your credit card company, but they won't care or do anything.
5. Cash is tangible. Counting it out to hand over to someone else makes you aware of how much you're spending.

I'm sure this system works for some financial avatars, but I hate using cash. Fumbling with my wallet and bills and coins and the receipt is stressful! Maybe that's weird.

Operation Use No Cash and Charge Everything You Can on Your Credit Card

Taking advantage of credit cards and treating them like a very short-term, zero-interest loan is one of the best ways to help your financial avatar. Credit cards are one of life's joys. The quick and easy swipe of the plastic. No fumbling!

Credit Card Chuck is another player in Mimi's financial life. He's actually quite generous at heart, appearing whenever Mimi needs anything and assuring the merchant that Mimi will pay for her need. He vouches for her.

Don't take advantage of his vouching though by making him look like a fool in front of the merchant. Pay Chuck back in full the first time he asks.

For Mimi, it's a perk John Cash and Mayor Civil make available to her. Pay it off in full when it's due and thank Chuck profusely for the short-term, no-interest loan.

List of reasons credit cards are better than cash
1. Protection. If you lose your wallet or it gets stolen, you can call Chuck, and he goes looking for it. You don't lose anything except your time on the phone call.
2. No juggling coins and bills while people behind you get annoyed with how slow you are.
3. It's easier to look at your purchases later. Everything is neatly listed online.

4. Sometimes credit card companies will give you miles to use on airlines for opening an account with them. Other credit cards will give you cash back or other perks.
5. It eliminates the need to find your specific bank's location to get cash out without paying a fee. Most places take credit cards without a fee.
6. If you have a dispute with a merchant and you put his wares on your credit card, the credit card company can suspend payment while they investigate. Chuck mediates the dispute. Another reason to protect his trust.

Operation Don't Use Your Debit Card Because Using a Debit Card for Purchases is Dumb

I use my debit card only to retrieve cash, so not using it for a month was a super easy operation, and I only brought it up to talk about debit cards. No mincing words here. Using a debit card to buy anything is stupid.

Debit card enthusiasts point out the card's convenience. No fumbling with your cash! Look at purchases online! You can spend only what you have!

Eh.

Credit cards link directly to the bank's money while debit cards link directly to *your* money. And banks treat your money very differently than they treat their money.

If someone steals your credit card before you realize it, you have a bit of time before it becomes a big problem. When you do realize it, hopefully in a day or so, and you alert the credit card company—Hey! Someone has been spending your money without your permission!—Chuck locks down the compromised account, sets you up with a new account, and sends you a new credit card while he investigates.

But if someone steals your debit card and you don't realize it before the thief uses it, oh dear. You alert the debit card company—Hey! Someone has been spending my money without my permission! They'll lock the compromised account and try to sort it, sure. But it's *your account*. You won't have access to your money while they investigate.

And if you have a dispute with a merchant after putting his wares on your debit card? Bummer. You just have to stew because he's already taken your actual money out of your actual account. It's like using cash. Merchant has final say after he pockets your money. There's no Chuck to help.

Debit cards aren't really that convenient. What if the balance in your account is precariously low? Aren't you constantly doing math to figure out how much you can spend so as not to overdraw the thing? Sounds like a huge pain. Don't some banks charge you money if your balance goes below $0?

Operation Don't Buy Anything New
Not buying anything new for a month is super easy. You can hold off on almost everything for only twenty-eight to thirty-one days. It forces you to think creatively and not just mindlessly purchase. Make it a game. A choice. A challenge.

Out of toothpaste? Dig through your cabinets and finish the half-used travel toothpaste in your travel bag.

A part of your car just ended its useful life and needs replacement? Try the bus or other public transportation until the month is over. Carpool with a friend and give him gas money. Hitchhike. Find a part on Craigslist or at a junkyard.

I added the caveat "new" in this operation to hone my skills at finding good used stuff. You'd be surprised by how much is out there.

Hold off on your purchases just a wee bit longer. It makes you appreciate them when you do get them.

Operation Window Shop Every Weekend and Try to See Why People Enjoy Shopping
Shopping every weekend and noting the prices of stuff can alert you to good deals by knowing what's out there. You'll know when to stock up on stuff you need.

My conclusion: I don't care. I hate shopping. I'll go to

the mall with you to walk around and get ten thousand steps in for the day, but please don't ask me to look for some shoes with you.

I don't shop online. Or peruse catalogs. I dislike wandering around stores without a specific purchase in mind. There is so much more in life to see and do and touch and be yelled at for touching. I don't want to spend my days looking at stuff to buy.

But that's me! Maybe you love to shop and doing this operation would give you ideas on how to shop without spending too much. Or how to shop and find deals for the future. Or something. I don't know how you can like shopping.

Operation Don't Eat Out Except if You're Ordering In and Eating at Your Desk

Don't eat out for a month and see how much you save. I bet it's a lot. I worked too much during the month I tried this operation and ate most of my meals at my desk. Work paid for that. Maybe I should have tried this operation again during a less stressful month, but I didn't. I can't do it now because I don't have a desk. Because I'm retired. Woot!

It's a good operation for you to try, though. If you're anything like me, you eat out a lot, and it quickly adds up. Preparing your meals at home is a super-obvious way to save money. Plus, it's probably healthier.

Operation Clean Out Your Pantry and Create Meal Plans

This is a fun clutter-clearing operation. I love clearing clutter as you know. So satisfying! Figure out what you have in your pantry and use it! Use it up! It feels really great. Cleaning out your cabinet will also help you save on your grocery bill. You know what you have and where it is.

Whenever I did this operation, I would also tend to eat out less and prepare more meals at home.

Operation Try the Generic Brands to See if You Can Tell the Difference

Did you know that a lot of generic store brands are exactly the same as the expensive, fancy, and familiar label brand? They use the same ingredients, the same factories, the same workers. Only the label and the price are different.

Some generics are not the same as the fancy label. When you swap all your preferences out for a month, you can see which ones are okay to substitute and which ones make you shudder in disgust.

Operation Don't Buy Drinks When You're Out and About

Drinks are often the most expensive part of a meal out. Especially alcohol. If you make it a point to stick with the complimentary water, you'll be saving a boatload. Maybe two boatloads. You still get to be eating and socializing, so it's a win all around.

Operation Cut Down Your Electric Bill By at Least 33.33333%

Shut off the cable box each night. Use free air to dry your clothes instead of the dryer. Don't watch TV. Run your dishwasher at night when the electricity is cheaper. Get an energy efficiency check. A lot of electric companies will offer them for free on occasion. Honestly, there are so many ways to cut down your electric bill.

Operation Bike to Work, You Lazy Slob

If you can live close enough to walk / bike / use public transportation efficiently to navigate to work and a grocery store, you should seriously consider ditching your car. Try biking instead.

I'm including my love of biking here because it saves money first and foremost. It's pretty much free after you fund a few small items.

My commute to work in Chicago using the L cost me $80/month for an unlimited pass. This expense was begging to be cut back, just pleading to be eliminated because Chicago, for the most part, is a beautifully flat city with bike lanes up the wazoo. At least, it had bike lanes from my apartment to my office building downtown, which is what matters. So I started *Operation Bike to Work, You Lazy Slob.*

Over the course of a few months, I claimed an old pink Huffy bike in my parents' garage (free), found a mechanic who fixed it up (bartered with him, so $0), nabbed a couple of locks from my parents' basement (free), and purchased a helmet ($20).

Shortly after my first successful commute to work, I canceled my monthly unlimited transit pass and made back the money I spent in a week. There were a gazillion weeks after that where my commute cost me nothing. Nothing!

A lot of cities have bike-sharing programs, so maybe try those if you don't want to spend money on an actual bike straight off. Many cities also offer free courses on bike maintenance, repair, and routes. Seriously, look into it. We're all here to help you. If you are relatively close to where you want to go, you can bike there at least some of the time, huh?

I like biking, but my favorite mode of transportation is walking. I love walking more than I love anything and will gladly walk anywhere for as long as you want.

Leisurely stroll to the library? Cool, which one? Date in Logan Square? Okay, I'll take the train to you and you can walk me back home. Meeting with a friend in Bridgeport? Argh, I just missed my bus, so will be about twenty minutes late. Sorry.

Unfortunately, walking allows you only so big a radius of wandering before you concede to time difficulties. After a couple of weeks of successful biking to work without dying, I realized that I could ride my bike all over the city.

Like everywhere. To do everything. My world opened up with my patented explosion noise. Biking easily triples the distance I can cover over walking.

Quick trip to the library to drop off books? That is like a three-minute detour on my way home from work. Date in Logan Square? Yes, there's a bike lane all the way there and all the way back! Meeting with a friend in Bridgeport? What better way to demonstrate the power of thrift than spending $0 to get there—and on time to boot!

I had a mode of transportation that I could control that was fast and convenient and so fast. I'm a big fan of the illusion of control.

Biking is a good way to supplement public transportation, walking, and yes, I guess, if you need to, your car. Think about it this way—cut down your car use enough and you can get rid of it. For the occasional times you do need four wheels, just use a car-sharing service like Zipcar. Or Uber.

After you've done a few of these Operations, you'll start to refine your system and understand what works for you. What is easy to let go of? What is much harder? You make the rules. Make it a game you can win.

How do you hold yourself accountable?
Set some goals

I'm a goal-orientated freakazoid. It's immensely satisfying to cross off a specific, attainable goal and then point my finger at the piece of paper and delight to myself, "I did that!"

I like to delight myself, so I've developed a bit of a checklist for making and crossing off goals.

Refine the goal. Words matter. Phrasing matters. The more concrete and clear the goal, the easier to reach. Don't write down nonsense goals like save money or retire early. What the heck does that even mean? Be specific. Pay off all my student loans. Generate enough passive income to cover my expenses. Okay, I know exactly what that means. Let's do this!

Word it so that you can control the result, an inner goal versus an outer goal. "Have enough money to make my friends jealous." Bad. "Have enough money so I don't worry about money." Better. "Generate enough passive income to cover my expenses." Best.

Create little subgoals. The goals worth anything are usually pretty big, so I try to break the dream down into smaller dreams. Pick one loan to pay off. Find one city where I could live with my current passive income. Make these goals achievable in the short-term to keep you focused on the long-term. Keep it manageable.

The purpose of making subgoals is give you an excuse to celebrate the progress. Don't focus so much on the destination that you forget it's a journey. Occasionally, take a minute to appreciate how far you've come. Get out of the car. Stretch your feet. Take in the vista.

Don't compare yourself to anyone else. Compare yourself to where you were a year ago. Are you improving? Is life getting better?

When you realize that you have control over a lot of the little things, the bigger goals seem a lot less scary. Human brains have a tendency to overestimate what they can accomplish in a day, but underestimate what they can accomplish in a year. Play the long game and change what you do one day at a time.

One of my favorite websites is FutureMe.org. Here you can write a letter to yourself and pick a date to have it delivered to your email account. I try to write a letter every month or so because I *love* receiving emails from the past.

Here is an excerpt of one from 2011-Anita.

Hello Dear,
You're sad and you're frustrated. Because it's past three a.m. and you're still at work, and you're rather an incompetent little fuzzball.

Are you out of debt yet? Does it feel awesome? $42,685 left.

I wish I were you.

-Me

I danced my debt-free jig long ago, but receiving that email pointed out that it wasn't always this way. We acclimate pretty quickly. I like the reminder. I need the reminder. **Find a way to measure the goal.** How will you know when you can schedule your victory parade if you're not measuring it? Personally, I don't have intuitive self-monitoring skills and need a visual aid I can point to frantically when self-doubt begins her inevitable grilling.

Measuring is fun though. You manage what you measure. Or, put another way, you *can't* manage what you don't measure. Manage it. Oversee it. Rule it. Create a visual aid that you can update as you make progress towards your goal. Use a spreadsheet or an app or a chart.

The daily eye candy will keep you motivated. The constant reminder of the prize—the specific attainable prize—will help you put the notions into action.

Keep yourself accountable. Everyone can have an expensive month and slip up. When you experience the thrill of a thrifty month and how much closer it brings you to your goal compared to the pain of an indulgent month, you start to change your behavior.

Hopefully.

Make time for your goals. Decide what you want to do and schedule it in. If it's important, you'll find the time.

If you're not making enough time for it, take a second and decide if this particular goal warrants your precious NOW. Overwhelmed with another project? Okay. Do the bare minimum and revisit the larger goal when you're ready. It's not always going to be linear.

I didn't pay that much attention to my student loans at first. My firm gave me a paid deferral year to ride out the 2009 recession, and I spent *just* enough time making sure I was paying the minimums each month. I even paid late once because I couldn't access the website abroad. The horror!

I still wanted to retire early, but my *See The World* Bucket List item claimed the majority of my mental energy and finances. I didn't seriously tackle *Operation Get Rid of that Debt, Man* until I started working as a lawyer. And then I made the time. Each month, I made sure to spend at least two days (the fifteenth and the last day of the month) calculating how much of my paycheck I could transfer to which loan and how much less in interest I could pay. Honestly, though, for the year I spent on *Operation Deb*t, I crunched those numbers daily.

Keep a resolutions chart

In *The Happiness Project*, Gretchen Rubin recommends keeping a chart of all your resolutions to help you accomplish your goals. Benjamin Franklin did something similar back in his day. In my case, I keep a spreadsheet with a list of any actions I want to make habits, any current operations I'm working on, subgoals, reminders, etc.

At the end of the day, if I've done the thing I'm supposed to have done, I find the square on my spreadsheet that corresponds to the activity and I type in a smiley face. I love those smileys.

It's kind of my master list and how I steer the ship of my life. It's my entertainment, my reason for waking, and my buddy. Here is a smattering of some of the items I've used for my chart.

Occasional resolutions for my chart

1. Make a to-do list
2. Don't eat out
3. Do some sort of physical activity, you lazy slob
4. Take a picture and put it on the Instagram
5. Write for two hours
6. Floss
7. Avoid time wasters
8. Read

9. Wear lotion
10. Wear sunscreen
11. Practice the evening tidy up, you lazy slob
12. Operation NYC, Yeah You Know Me
13. Be generous
14. Tackle a nagging task
15. Wear makeup
16. Be frugal
17. Don't eat alone
18. Stop calling yourself a lazy slob
19. Meditate
20. Take Vitamin D

This list is much, much longer, but you get the picture.

My resolutions chart helped me evaluate the various money-saving operations I told you about earlier in this chapter. A lot of smiley faces in that column meant Mimi probably liked that system.

Fewer smiley faces meant Mimi didn't love the strategy. If you find yourself floundering at any stage, go back and refine your words. Be more specific. Be less specific. Go a different direction. Make it a goal you *like* to keep. Then you'll be able to keep it easily. That's why I harped on the wording. Words matter, dammit.

It's about accountability. What are you trying?

Attitude matters. Expectations matter. Not just with

money, but everything in life. I love my resolutions chart with all my soul, but it does give me a very glaring account of my flaws. I always fail so miserably at "avoid time-wasters." I wish I had never discovered how amazing I am at FreeCell. I'm too good not to play it. It's a real problem.

Cultivate a system

I understand if chasing goals makes you feel like you're constantly failing. That's what a goal *is*—a very specific objective that you can very possibly fail miserably at. I counter this feeling by creating a system to supplement my goals. Adopt as much vocabulary as you can to train your brain.

A system is a deliberate activity that you do regularly just because you know your life will be better if you make it a habit. You don't have a specific end in mind; you just know that overall shit improves when you do it.

I preach about goals because I nailed a goal that made me feel tingly. Now I look back only with fondness on *Operation Get Rid of That Debt, Man*. That final payment felt like shackles lifted, an elephant stepped off my chest, and now it's time to dance! Yes!

I find most goals fall somewhere in between those two extremes of utter failure (FreeCell) and easy success (retiring early). It's probably just semantics. But I love words. Words matter. Framing matters.

Goal: Pay off that loan
System: Don't buy crap you don't need

Goal: Save enough money so your passive income covers your expenses
System: Don't buy crap you don't need

The reason I nailed the financial goals so quickly was because I used a system that made sense to me. Why waste your resources on stuff?

By the law of averages, we are average at most things. We are below average at some things. We are above average at some things. Figure out the thing you like doing and that you're good at and go do that. You are what you do every day. Fill your days with the things you love to do and you'll love your life. At least this seems to be working for me.

Goal: Write a book
System: Write

Goal: See the entire world
System: Travel

Goal: What's the end?
System: Make it the journey

Use all the words to train your attitude and your actions. Control what you can. Shrug off what you can't.

Buck up

You're going to get lost at some point. Expect it. Sometimes annoying things will occur and set you back. You're not going to be good at everything you try, and not everything will work for you.

When I don't try, I always fail. But even when I do try, I still often fail. So what? Everybody fails. When you keep going in spite of the failure, you're doing better than most of the people out there. Showing up and trying repeatedly is the hard part. Grittiness.

I know this sounds simple, but all of my advice is simple. Remind yourself of why you made that decision when the moping starts. Feel empowered. Take out your map, and look at where you want to go. Believe that what you're doing matters to your financial avatar.

Tell yourself that you get up and go to work because you decided you're going for financial independence. (Or whatever your current goal is.)

Nobody is making you do anything. You want a bigger life. The bigger dream. You know things will get better tomorrow because you're always trying to get better.

Check out your chart, and see how well you're doing. Only nine more days until the next paycheck. Only $1,809 on that Perkins loan. Yeah! Remember that you have power and complete control.

Or rather, remember that you have complete control over the second category of the axis of control. Your attitude. Your reaction. Hopefully your decisions. Focus on that sweet spot. After you find what you like to do, make that the thing you repeatedly do. Cultivate your systems in this space. Showing up is a lot easier if you like what you're showing up for. Getting up is a lot easier when you're excited about the thing you're getting up for.

Don't get discouraged with the occasional detour while looking for what you like. Think of the experience as one more data point you've collected. Start a list entitled *Shit my financial avatar hates*, wipe your brow, and then try something else. It doesn't matter what you do, only *that* you do.

Do you advocate for yourself?

Nobody cares about your money as much as you do. If you don't take care of it and nurture its superpowers, who's going to do it for you? Not me.

Little purchases matter. Big purchases matter. How much you make matters. Everything matters. It's your attitude about money and your system of how you live your life.

Increasing your income *and* reducing your expenses grows your capital even faster. You don't have complete control over how much money you make, but you can learn how to negotiate and jump up that range.

My rule of thumb is always negotiate when it comes to salary and benefits. Most of the time, or at least some of the time, the salary offer initially on the table is only the starting point. Isn't the possibility worth the request?

The worst outcome that will arise is that your potential future employer says no and you have to re-evaluate. And if there *is* a negative repercussion from merely asking for more money, that tells you a lot about how the company values its employees and is a good lesson on bullet dodging.

So how do you negotiate? Speak confidently and know your worth. Intelligently discuss your request with data and numbers to back up your position.

I gave you my brief financial life summary in the introduction but omitted a few months for brevity and because I knew I'd talk about them here. In early 2006, I quit one workers' compensation claims-handler job for a second workers' compensation claims-handler job. I was restless and eager for change, contemplating a new life. A recruiter happened to call me on the right day, so I interviewed and received an offer. I sent the recruiter the email below, asking for more money. I dug through my Gmail account to find this, so it really is the actual email (stupid typo and all) with key details redacted:

Hi [Recruiter],

I crunched all the numbers this weekend, and although it's a very tempting offer, I will have to decline if the salary isn't raised. I've only been working for 3 years, but every year, I get extremely high reviews and large raises, so I know I'm making pretty good money right now. My exact salary is $53,100 after my review about a month ago. They match 7% of the 401k at $0.85/dollar. For the first year at [potential employer], I would make:

[Potential Employer]: $55,000 − $90/month for insurance = $53,920.

Whereas, if I stayed at [Current Employer] that year, it would be:

[Current Employer]: $53,100 + $3159.45 (matched 401k) − $108.00 for medical, vision, dental insurance = $56,151.45.

I also have to take into account the discount I get on my car insurance from working here. On the 3 cars my parents and I own, it's discounted nearly $800. Plus, I get 2 days off per month at [Current Employer], whereas I would only get 1 at [Potential Employer]. The $3159.45 from my 401k grows at (very conservative estimate) 4% per year. I'm only 23, so that is a good chunk of change in 40 years.

I was very impressed w/the company and the people seem very nice, but I can't take a step down in my career pay-wise at this point. If the offer is upped to $60,000, I will take it. I understand that is a significant jump and they will be unlikely to offer that much, but I can't justify taking walking away from [Current Employer] for any less.

Kind Regards,

Anita

That email worked and they increased their offer. I don't remember how much it was exactly, but I know it was at least close to the full amount, if not the full amount.

Want another example? When my law firm asked if I wanted to move to Sydney, my initial reaction was, "Yes! Holy crap, yes! When do I leave?" They offered me a cost of living adjustment, and again my brain shouted, "Yes! Holy crap, yes! WHY HAVEN'T I LEFT YET?"

But I resisted that impulse, kept my mouth shut, and ran more numbers. I couldn't find the actual email I sent because I used my work email account that no longer exists, but here is my best attempt at a re-creation.

Yo yo yo HR lady,

I am so thrilled about the offer and the prospect of moving to Sydney. What a dream!

Alas! I am having a bit of trouble reconciling the numbers. The cost of living in Chicago is amazingly affordable. While I understand that the cost of living adjustment proposed would be a wonderful deal for someone in the New York office to move to Sydney, for me, it would be a terrible financial decision.

The rent alone in Sydney doubles the entirety of my Chicago expenses. I checked. A fun fact about Australia is that a lot of apartments don't come with refrigerators or washing machines! I'd have to buy those myself. I also have to replace all my other appliances because the voltages are different. Part of the appeal of moving to Australia is that it's on the other side of the world! But that also means if I ever wanted to see my family, I'd need to buy an expensive flight.

Have you checked the exchange rate lately? The Australian dollar is very strong right now and has been steadily getting stronger. It's nearly on par with the US dollar! I'm hoping there is some wiggle room here and you can consider my request.

Cheers,

Anita

I didn't receive the entire amount I asked for, but that email *did* net me an increased cost of living adjustment and a one-time moving allowance in my first paycheck in Sydney to offset the cost of new appliances. Woooooot!

It doesn't hurt to ask. Also, it always helps if you're prepared to walk away. The most valuable thing money can buy is freedom from worrying about money. I know I repeat that a lot, but it perfectly encapsulates how to think about money. If you're not living paycheck to paycheck and are master of your cash, you have a lot more room to negotiate. Remember the wiggle room? You won't feel obligated to take the first offer that comes along. You'll know your worth and your potential future employer will also understand your worth.

I was fully prepared to stay at my first insurance job if they didn't accept my counteroffer as I was already considering law school. I was also fully prepared to move to Sydney for less money than I received for the firm job because it was the lure of the adventure.

Money gives you the freedom to make your life what you want it to be. Remember that money is a tool to help you live the life you want to live. Know yourself well enough to know what life will make you happy.

Case in point, despite getting an increased offer, my stint at the second insurance company in early 2006 lasted only a couple of months. Soon after starting this new job that came with more money but no more happiness, I saw an advertisement for a small charter airline that needed flight attendants. I interviewed and when I received an offer, I immediately accepted without a peep.

This fact may or may not surprise you, but the pay for an air hostess was substantially less than I made in insurance, but I never for a second considered saying no because of that. I didn't request more money because I just wanted the experience. The promise of adventure made up for the decrease in compensation. Money isn't everything. Money just gives you the freedom to make your life what you want it to be. And, at that point, I wanted to be a flight attendant.

You have more control over this stuff than you realize. What you don't have control over is time. It's relentlessly ticking by. Are you happy with your days?

ACTION PLAN!
PLAN YOUR CALENDAR

Step 1: Make a list of six different month-long operations you want to try, and decide when you're going to do them. Put them on your calendar.

Step 2: Until you get to net worth zero, calculate and update your net worth once a week. Put a reminder on your calendar. If you're feeling ambitious, it could be daily. It shouldn't take more than a couple of minutes because you've already done all the leg work in previous action plans.

If you're net worth is already positive, recalculate it at the end of each month. Put a reminder on your calendar.

Step 3: Start a resolutions chart with at least five money-related resolutions. Spend a few minutes each day giving yourself a smiley face if you kept it.

Step 4: Put a reminder on your calendar to write yourself a letter to the future at futureme.org every month.

Step 5: Do the activities as they come up on your calendar.

CHAPTER 4

How Should I Invest?

AFTER YOU KNOW how to save the money you earn, make that money work for you. The world will always need capital. It takes money to do everything and anything. If you have excess money to lend to people so they can do the shit they want to do, you're in for a happy life.

Are you borrowing money? Or are you lending money? I hope it's obvious what label is preferable.

Do you know about compound interest? Are you using it correctly?
Poor people stay poor and get poorer by using compound interest as a crutch. They don't have wiggle room, so when they find themselves in a bind, they borrow money at outrageous interest rates. On the flip side, rich people stay rich and get richer by using compound interest as a ladder. They invest and their money grows.

Like money, compound interest is just another fact of life and another character my financial avatar interacts with that can be either rude or polite. I'd like you to meet Compound Interest Charlie. He's a robot from Cleveland.

When I was paying down my student loans, Mimi used to think he was evil. He would knock on her door or find her when she was at the library and then take some of her money. It was frustrating, to say the least.

What Mimi didn't understand, because she was a baby, is that CI Charlie is just a robot doing his job. Each morning, he whizzes out of his robot dormitory and pulls out a clipboard with a giant frowny face on it and a single name underneath. He finds the person whose name he reads on the list and takes that person's money. Predictably, the financial avatars involved are very annoyed.

Each afternoon though, the mood changes. Around 2 pm, Charlie whips out his clipboard again. This time the clipboard has a giant thumb pointing upwards on it along with a name underneath. Charlie finds the person whose name he read on the afternoon list, but this time, the encounter is much more fun. He gives that person some money. The financial avatars involved are positively giddy.

But CI Charlie doesn't care. Morning and afternoon are the same for him. The names mean nothing to him. He has no emotion. He's a robot. To make the interaction with CI Charlie pleasant, your financial avatar just needs to hop from the list with the unhappy visage to the list with the happy thumb.

After I paid off my student loans, I started to invest. Now when Charlie knocks on Mimi's door, it's a delight because he's there to give her money. Mimi considers Charlie a close friend. Charlie considers Mimi nothing because he's a robot and can't consider.

It all starts with your income and expenses.

Let's say you're a chronic overspender and every month you find yourself in need of just ten more dollars. You go to Charlie, and he loans you the $10, but interest accumulates in the meantime to the tune of 20%, compounding monthly. Now he's terrorizing your financial avatar.

Compounding interest, man! This really stinks.

By the time he comes back the next month, you owe him $12. If, throughout that month, you overspent again by ten dollars, you need to borrow more. Oh well. You don't change your life at all, and, at the end of the year, Charlie demands almost $500 from you even though you borrowed only $120.

That was me when I was paying down my student loans, except that second month when I owed $12, I followed my rules on how to spend money and underspent for the month. Underspending meant I could give Charlie an extra dollar instead of borrowing ten more.

When you're done paying off your debts and you're still underspending, here comes the good part. You go to Charlie and loan him the money. He promises you an interest rate of 7%, compounded monthly.

By the time he comes back next month, he hands you $10.70. Since you have another excess $10 from this month, you give that to him along with the $10.70 he tried to give you. At the end of the year, Charlie knocks on your door with nearly $200 even though you gave him only $120.

Compounding interest, man! This really rocks.

That's me now. Living off compound interest.

Spend less than you earn and invest the difference. Earn interest on the interest on the interest on the interest on the interest (you get the idea). It builds on itself. Or spend more than you earn and borrow the difference. Then you pay interest on the interest on the interest on the interest on the interest on the interest on the…

The spiffy part about compound interest is the compounding part. The hole of debt gets deeper and deeper or the mountain of money gets higher and higher.

Oh, and that 20% Charlie charges is actually less than what many credit cards charge. The 7% is what I expect to receive annually, on average, from my investment vehicle of choice.

Money is powerful! Compound interest is powerful! Do you want them working for you or against you?

For you. The answer is for you.

How should I invest?

So, how do you harness the power of compound interest? When you're working and accumulating, what do you buy with your excess money?

Bonds? Land? Stocks? Amethysts? Stuff it all under the mattress?

I'm only joking about that last option, of course. The idea of keeping everything in cash might sound safe, but inflation will almost certainly eat away at your buying power. The current interest rates on savings accounts are rather abysmal. Keeping your wealth in cash won't let you take advantage of compound interest.

I was only joking about the amethysts as well. I'm not going to invest in gold bars and a safe deposit box either. That seems to go against my "stuff is bad" instinct.

In my opinion, the best option would be high-interest, safe, long-term bonds. *Your Money or Your Life* recommends buying government treasury bonds. At the time, that was a good suggestion. You knew exactly what the long-term interest rate was, and that long-term rate was decent. And that long-term interest rate was pretty much guaranteed, so there was minimal risk involved.

Sounds awesome, right? Unfortunately, by the time I was ready to start investing in 2011, buying government treasury bonds would not shorten my working life. The long-term interest rate stank for investors. The return for safe bonds was too low.

What about stocks? I like the idea of stocks, putting money towards companies creating something, owning a piece of their success and a stake in their future.

But which stocks are going to perform well and which stocks represent companies that will not do well? I don't know. You don't either. Nobody does. And anyone who tells you they do know is a con artist or delusional. Or both.

Since I have no idea which companies are going to perform well in the future, my solution is to bet on everything. The total stock market index fund. It's a collection of stocks. A whole bunch of stocks. All the stocks. It's the best strategy out there. In my opinion.

All of the investment greats recommend this investment strategy. Warren Buffett. John Bogle. JL Collins. Me.

My specific investment vehicle of choice is called VTSAX. It stands for the Vanguard Total Stock Market

Index Fund. Here is what VTSAX's prospectus said about this fund's investment strategy in April 2017:

> The Fund employs an indexing investment approach designed to track the performance of the CRSP US Total Market Index, which **represents approximately 100% of the investable U.S. stock market** and includes large-, mid-, small-, and micro-cap stocks regularly traded on the New York Stock Exchange and Nasdaq. *(Emphasis mine.)*[8]

Basically, I invest in every single company that one can buy in the United States. I'm betting on society, on progress, on civilization, on you, on everything. I'm betting that we prosper and continue to invent and create and strive. That's my optimism.

Sure, some companies lose money and go bankrupt. But that just makes my fund self-cleansing. If a company is no longer viable, it stops existing and stops dragging down my fund. Meanwhile other companies make more money than they know what to do with and distribute it to me in the form of dividends.

This strategy isn't risk-free, but nothing is risk-free. You could choke on the next piece of gum you chew. What are you going to do? Give up gum?

Personally, I find alternative strategies scarier. I've

investigated and dismissed the alternatives. Real property doesn't appeal to me even a tiny bit right now. I'll tell you why soon. Bonds might sound fun in a couple of decades. Cash will only dwindle.

The riskiest alternative of all: paying someone else to guess which magic collection of stocks is going to outperform the rest. I may hand over a few dollars to a persuasive reader of palms at a carnival for laughs, but I'm not going to pay someone to guess which companies are going to perform well. Actually, I probably wouldn't even do the carnival thing.

You can spend hours studying charts and trying to find patterns, poring over financial disclosures and prognosticating which companies will be desired and groundbreaking at some point in the future. And people do! They tout their investment knowledge and charge people money to use their guesses.

If you knew when to time the market, you'd be a fast billionaire. And psychic. An actively managed mutual fund or a day trader can have a lucky year and beat the total stock market occasionally, but it is impossible to do so consistently and over the long run. But since these guys are spending their time reading the tea leaves, they expect payment for their fund of guesses.

Regardless of how well they guessed, in good years and bad, they will extract a percentage of your money for their own pockets. They tell you about these fees in their reports. It's not illegal. Just stupid.

Fees are the worst. I try to do business with any company that minimizes fees. That's why I chose Vanguard. When you buy a Vanguard fund, you become a shareholder of Vanguard. When Vanguard makes money, you make money. Vanguard is the only investment company that I know of that uses this model. Hence Vanguard has the lowest fees. And low fees make a big difference.

And before you ask, no, I'm not a shill for Vanguard. I wish I were a shill. That would be so fun. But, no. We're not even in the same league. If we were in high school, Vanguard wouldn't even notice me, much less ask me to dance at prom.

Can I introduce you to two more characters in my financial avatar's world? First is Norm.

Norm is alternative-universe Mimi. He buys everything Mimi doesn't and tells Mimi about it in great detail.

And Charlotte.

Charlotte runs a psychic hotline and Norm calls often, wanting to know exactly what mix of tech and fertilizer companies will make big profits. In return for her knowledge, Charlotte charges a measly 1% per year. She assures Norm that he'll be making so much money, he won't even notice the fee.

Norm gives Charlotte $10,000. Mimi buys $10,000 of VTSAX. The expense ratio fee for this fund is 0.05%. I'll be generous and say that Charlotte did as well as my precious VTSAX.

They both get a 7% rate of return, but Mimi's effective rate of return is 6.95% while Norm's is 6%.

After 20 years, Mimi has more than $38,000 while Norm has just over $32,000. The cost to invest was $6,265.44 higher for Norm. That's 60% of the initial investment! 62.6544% of the initial investment, to be exact.

Even tenths of a percent matter given compound interest and time.

If we don't give Charlotte the benefit of the doubt and assume that's she's like every other investment adviser out there, she does worse than the total market. She studies company earnings and performs rain dances and picks a mix of companies she thinks are going to do well in the future. Perhaps some years she may beat VTSAX. Maybe.

But most of the time she doesn't. And she still takes the 1% fee regardless of how she does. Even if she decimates Norm's portfolio, he still has to pay her the fee.

Nobody has consistently beaten the total stock market because nobody can predict the future. When you do use an actively managed mutual fund or day trade, the expenses nibble at your returns in both the good and bad years.

A rising tide lifts all boats and a tsunami destroys all ships. If VTSAX were to collapse, there would be something seriously bad happening in the world, and I'm guessing I'd have bigger things to worry about.

A buy and hold strategy of the total stock market index fund is the best method to consistently make money.

How will you know when you have enough?

Operation Enough! means having enough money to last you for the rest of your life, but not so much money that you waste too much of your time on this planet accumulating it doing something that doesn't make you happy.

I like having a visual aid that I can gaze at when I'm feeling jittery. Yes, I have enough. This pretty chart tells me I do.

Your Money or Your Life recommends making a retirement chart to help you figure out when you have enough. I'm echoing their brilliance and recommending you do the same. First, the easy stuff. Each month, plot your expenses (the long-dotted line) and your income (the short-dotted line). The bigger the gap between the two, the better off you are. What's your savings rate?

Here's my chart after I'd been working as a lawyer for a couple of years.

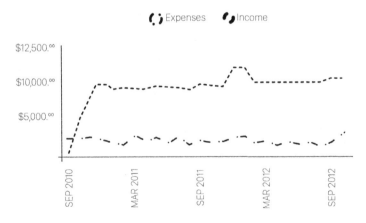

Maximize the amount of space between the short-dotted line and the long-dotted line. That gap is your savings.

Yes, I know. *My* gap is ridiculous. That's why I was on the super mega fast track to retirement.*

When I started working as a lawyer, my net worth had been negative. I had more in student loans than I did in my 401(k) retirement account from before law school.

Now the slightly more complicated stuff. My theoretical projected passive income line—the solid fella below.

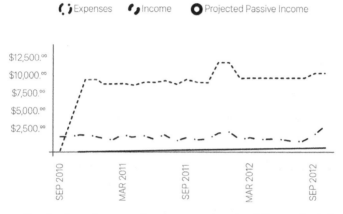

I calculate this number using a method I tweaked from *Your Money or Your Life*. The formula in the book reads:

$$[(\text{capital}) \times (\text{current long-term interest rate})] / 12 = \text{monthly investment income}$$

---

* I need to tell you that some of the numbers are approximate. I didn't keep meticulous track of my expenses until March 2011 and my net worth is approximate until January 2012. Aging avatars meant utilizing different tools. With my financial avatar baby, I used more brain cells on specific loans than worrying about my overall net worth. Everything after those dates is pretty accurate though. Heck, even the approximations are pretty good. Also, these are illustrated recreations of the actual charts on my blog.

As I mentioned earlier, I don't invest in bonds because their long-term interest rate right now is cruddy. I invest in stocks. Stocks don't have a set long-term rate of return though, so I had to tweak the formula for myself. Instead of using the interest rate, I use withdrawal rate.

[(net worth) x (estimated yearly withdrawal rate)] / 12 = monthly projected passive income

What's a safe withdrawal rate? I don't know, but I use 4%.

I took that number from some finance professors working at Trinity University. In the 90s, these dudes decided to take a look at stock and bond returns from 1926 through 1997. I like the time frame they picked. 1929 is when the stock market collapsed and kicked off the Great Depression. That was a rough time. 1997 is close to when they initially published the article, so I'm guessing that's the last year they had complete data for.

They ran a variety of scenarios using differing mixes of stocks and bonds and calculated how much you could have theoretically taken out per year (your withdrawal rate) against the returns the investments gave you.

They came up with a lot of data and conclusions, but here are a few takeaways. At least, these were my takeaways. This takes inflation into account as well, so you could maintain your buying power. Success meant you had money in the investment account at the end of the time period.

1. If you invested in 100% stocks and lived on 3% of your investments each year, you were successful 100% of the time over a thirty-year period.
2. If you invested in 100% stocks and lived on 4% of your investments each year, you were successful 98% of the time over a thirty-year period.
3. If you invested in 100% stocks and lived on 5% of your investments each year, you were successful 81% of the time over a thirty-year period.

I picked 4% for my withdrawal rate for my own finances, and this is the number I use in my charts. If I take out 4% of my investments each year, most of the time, I will have enough money until I die. If the past is any indication, theoretically, my gamble will work out 98% of the time.

Theoretically! If the past is any indication! Those are very important caveats. The Trinity Study was based on what has happened in the past. If you've ever read a prospectus, you know the warnings splattered around the language touting the investment, "past performance is not indicative of future success." My VTSAX has that sentiment in its prospectus as well.

"Keep in mind that the Fund's past performance

(before and after taxes) does not indicate how the Fund will perform in the future."[9]

I love the jovial nature of that warning. I frequently drafted these types of documents when I lawyered. Of course the past is not a guarantee for the future. Nothing is. But the past is all we have to go on.

Maybe inflation will go to 2,000%. Perhaps the economy will enter into a decade-long stagnation. I don't know. What investment would be better in these cases? Does it make sense to plan for scary outcomes that have a small chance of occurring?

You can't plan for every scenario. I've tried; believe me. There are too many variables, and trying to plan for each one will only make you crazy. A giant rock could collide with our only habitable planet. A very intelligent yeti could hatch a diabolical plan to destroy humans. Maybe he's already been planning for months. Perhaps we'll go to war with West Virginia. Maybe climate change will kill us all.

These things are outside my axis of control, and I do my best not to worry about them. What's inside my axis of control is making the most informed decisions I can with the information available.

I use a lot of assumptions that may turn out to be horribly wrong. In fact, I'm willing to bet that at least one of my assumptions will end up being wrong. I assume that my investments will return, on average, 7% each year and inflation will be 3% each year. Thus, I can take out 4% and never touch the principal and maintain my buying power. On average. In an average year. The problem is that we don't know which years will be average until those years have already happened.

Plans are worthless; planning is everything. Even the authors of the Trinity Study point out, reasonably, that flexibility is key. This research is enough to assuage my anxiety, but not enough to just completely ignore my financial avatar. Remember, you manage what you measure.

Strap in for the ride

I should warn you that the market is going to fluctuate. That's what it does. Sometimes it goes temporarily up and sometimes it goes temporarily down.

If you're in the buying phase of your *Operation Enough!*, you *want* the market to drop. VTSAX is on sale! Celebrate the discount! Control your attitude about it.

When I was working and had a steady income, I kept roughly three months of living expenses in a checking account. This was my wiggle room. My paychecks funneled my average monthly expenses into that checking account and then funneled the remainder into my lovely VTSAX.

Whenever I noticed the market dipping, I would picture a big sale sticker on my VTSAX and would try to start the wave in excitement. As a thrifty person, I love sales.

HOW SHOULD I INVEST?

If you want to get "rich," you have to resist the urge to PANIC! and sell when your portfolio falls. Remember, the saying is "buy low and sell high" and not "buy as it's rising and panic-sell as it's dropping." If you want to get really rich, you have to not panic and you have to buy more when it's down. Double down and play the long game.

If you're in the buying phase and the market is up, check your balance in your investment account and cheer! Look at your net worth go! Whee! Control your attitude about it.

After you retire and don't have any income, the game changes a bit. When the market is up, you can continue to whee and watch your net worth increase while you eat a snack. When the market is temporarily down though, it's a bit harder. I think this is the reason why people work longer than they need to. It can be a terrifying ride on the market.

I believe in my philosophy and my investment advice 100%, but I'm not immune to anxiety. On the contrary, anxiety and I are tight. After I retired and I noticed the market was down that day, I shuddered with the realization that my net worth only decreased. I didn't have a surplus paycheck to take advantage of the low price and experienced only the full brutal fall.

I would be itching to buy more VTSAX. But I couldn't buy more because I didn't have a job because I refused to try to time the market. Based on that refusal, I gave up my guaranteed income to live and travel and write and generally be a bum.

Alternate-Universe Anita, who decided to keep working her lawyer job, likes to taunt me over her increasing net worth. I gleefully point out that I wake up whenever I want every single day. That often shuts her up.

I don't regret my decision, but it still kills me to roll my empty shopping cart past the orange stickers advertising a fire sale.

I handle this problem by ignoring it. The day-to-day fluctuations don't matter. More importantly, these day-to-day fluctuations are outside my axis of control.

I don't consider the drop a loss because I don't plan to sell all of my investments at once. I own shares in civilization and I have to have faith that civilization will continue to improve and any correction is merely another bump in the road like so many we've seen before.

Ever since the stock market's inception, more than one hundred years ago, the trend is clearly up.*

---

* Technically, this is the Dow Jones Industrial Average Index, which is not the *entire* stock market, but it's a good approximation. And a pretty chart. Also, this is an artist's rendering.

The trend has gone up through the stock market crash of 1929, the Great Depression, WWI, WWII, disco, the Korean War, the Vietnam War, my birth, your birth, the birth of the internet, the death of Michael Jackson, the impeachment of one president and resignation of another, the dotcom boom and bust, the Cold War, both Gulf Wars, the Great Recession, the Civil Rights Movement, and probably one or two other events I'm forgetting.

So that's the forest view. Big picture. Long term. The tree view is a little bit scarier. When you're in the trenches and day to day, it can be really gross to see the occasional drop in your investment. I have zero desire to look at my dwindling assets regularly when the market throws a temper tantrum and I don't need to. They're just numbers on a screen. I take out a small enough percentage of the total that it should be fine eventually. It should go back up eventually.

If you think civilization will continue, the stock market will go back up. And if civilization is ending, what investment would be safe? A hidden bunker?

So, this is what I do now post-retirement. Every four months, I schedule a fifteen-minute check-in with Mimi. The rest of the time I don't think about my finances. I don't check the market and obsess. I live my life. What a concept!

In those fifteen minutes, I check my credit scores. I add up my credit card bills from the past four months and the cash I took out in the past four months and then I take an average of those past four months. My expenses data point. I plot that number on my chart.

Then I take a peek at my investment accounts and calculate my theoretical projected passive income at that moment. If it's higher than the average monthly expenses I just calculated, I mutter reassuringly to myself and go about my life. If it's not higher…well, I haven't come across that scenario since retiring.

But I can adapt and be flexible. I can alter my extravagant lifestyle. Maybe I go hang out in a cheap country for a bit. Or work at Starbucks. I still have my legal degree. I don't think I threw that away.

Indeed, the deeper I wade into this early retirement

HOW SHOULD I INVEST?

thing, the more I think I would have to *actively try* to not make any more money.

That's my favorite piece of muttering reassurance.

If you're the type of person who is going for early retirement, I'm guessing you're capable, resourceful and open-minded. Especially if you're following your passion and getting better at it, you might have to actively try to not make any more money either.

This is my chart through April 2017, with just my expenses and projected passive income.

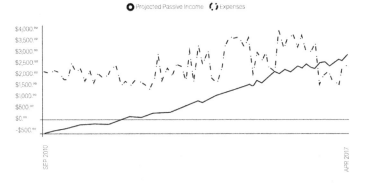

Looking at this makes me so tingly! Can you feel it? No? That's because it's my chart and not yours. After you've nursed your chart for several years, you'll understand my love.* As long as the solid line is higher than the long-dotted line, I can take off my worry pants. That's how I know I have enough.

I almost never think about money, much less worry

---

* I update my chart every four months on my blog at thepowerofthrift.com.

138

about it. I can't tell you what to do, only tell you what I do. If it helps, cool beans. If it doesn't help and you disagree, the beans are still cool.

ACTION PLAN!
PLOT AWAY

Step 1: Chart your income and your expenses for the last six months to a year. How are you doing?

Step 2: Add in the projected passive income line after you've started investing.

> [(Net worth) X (Withdrawal rate)]/12 = projected monthly passive income

Step 3: Put a calendar reminder to update it each month.

Step 4: Update once every four months after your projected passive income exceeds your expenses (once you retire).

What about Real Property?

Real property is property in the land-and-house-owning sense of the word. Personal property is everything else you can legally own (i.e. your stuff).

This section is not about buying real property strictly as an investment. You can buy, spruce up, flip, and make money. People do that. I'm not talking about real property to buy and rent out for other people to have a happy place to lay their heads at night. People do that, too. I know you can make money like that. This is not that type of book. I watch too much *Judge Judy*, and I have no desire to landlord or subcontract.

This analysis only applies to buying real property as a home for you and your family to have a happy place to lay your heads at night. Maybe someone you know has told you that it's silly to throw away money on rent, that buying the home you live in is a great investment. I'll admit that real property probably isn't a depreciating asset on the whole and you can make money on it if you're lucky, but I don't think buying a house is necessarily a smart financial move for everyone.

Don't get me wrong, my financial avatar gives money freely and happily for me to have a happy place to lay my head at night. This probably takes up the largest part of my budget, and I am more than okay with that. I'm happy to sign a lease for a nice apartment for eighteen months. I'm happy to pick out happy, sunny Airbnb places in different countries for a month. Happy to laze about in a hotel for a few nights. Happy, happy, happy.

It's the room-and-board piece of the happiness puzzle. You should spend money on housing, and you should spend it happily. I tell you this as a preface because I know you'll probably disagree with my point of view on the rest of this topic. That's okay. We can still be friends.

Here's my list of reasons for not buying real property.

(1) Real property is expensive. It's very likely the most expensive thing any of us have ever considered buying. For a significant chunk of your total net worth, you can have your name on a piece of paper in a basement office of some government building, proclaiming you responsible for your little slice of the earth.

(2) After forking over a significant chunk of your net worth, you still have to pay rent. Even if you own this real property completely and indisputably 100% outright, you really don't. You still have to pay some monthly amount to *someone* for your head's happy place. The government is going to tax you on that property every single year. Whether it's your landlord or your taxman, you will need some cash flow for "rent."

We're all renting. From Mother Earth. I know that's cheesy. I'm not deleting it.

So, here's a caveat because life is complicated. If you can find a good deal on real property and if the taxes and upkeep are less than you would pay for rent, then maybe you should buy the place you sleep in.

I don't necessarily oppose having your name on the paper. In fact, I almost bought real property once. In March 2012, a friend emailed me the listing of a one-bedroom, one-bathroom condo for sale in Chicago right across the street from where I lived.

At that time, twenty-nine-year-old-Anita, five glorious months into post-student-loan-debt life, was building up a balance that sat in a bank account and reading investment books, contemplating a path to financial independence. Like I said, *Your Money or Your Life* guided my thinking about money and my charts, but I wasn't sold on my older edition's investment advice.

I wasn't really considering buying an apartment, but the price tag—the product of a short sale—screamed at me. My commute to work was perfect. I loved my neighborhood. Cousins and a sister lurked around every corner. My plan at that point was to continue working at my firm in Chicago until I hit my financial goals, a prospect that was at least two years away.

The apartment showed well when I toured it, and I put in an offer for $70,000 cash. That figure represented a scary percentage of my net worth at that point, but my old 401(k) was chugging along as well, and I knew that I could quickly replenish it if I only stayed the course at my current job.

Most importantly, buying the condo would lower the monthly amount I paid for accommodations to only $350/month, for taxes and association fees. To put that number in perspective, over the years renting in various neighborhoods in Chicago, I paid anywhere from $750 to $1200 rent per month.

If you do this kind of math and analysis and you decide that real property is right for you, great! Invite me to your housewarming party. I'll bring champagne.

Plotting my own party, I transferred $1,000 earnest money into an account and waited for the bank to approve the short sale offer.

(3) Buying real property is complicated and (4) expensive. Since the idea of owning a specific location on earth is so fundamentally different from the items we typically buy and consume, there are a lot of rules and fees, and you need a whole cadre of people to navigate your way through this labyrinth.

You'll likely need a real estate agent to show you houses and a lawyer to review the paperwork. The paperwork. My god, the paperwork. You'll need to talk to banks and accountants and surveyors and inspectors.

If you want to buy real property, you not only need the

money for the actual property, but you also need money to pay for a lot of other things. Here's a list of possible expenses you may have to pay on top of the purchase price:

1. Title searches
2. Owner's title insurance if you like insurance
3. Transfer taxes
4. Recording fees for the deed
5. A home inspection to tell you of its flaws
6. A survey to tell you its exact boundaries
7. Legal fees for the cumbersome contracts
8. Homeowner's insurance

(5) Financing real property is complicated and (6) expensive. I had enough to pay for the condo outright, but I know that is an extremely rare occurrence. If you don't have the entire not-really-small chunk of change for the property up front, you have to get a mortgage!

A mortgage! You get to pay so much interest to the bank! Sure, the government lets you claim some money off your tax returns for this specific type of interest in a convoluted redistribution of wealth, but there are still fees galore for the pleasure of financing your new home. Here's a list of possible expenses the bank may make you pay:

1. Loan origination fees
2. Credit reports
3. Title insurance

4. Points
5. Flood life of the loan fee
6. PMI insurance
7. Appraisals

I'm not going to mention the interest you pay to the bank again because that math makes me uneasy. I know I just did. I'm not sorry.

(7) You have to pay to maintain it in the medium-term and long-term as long as your name is on it. I always do my best to maintain my tiny slice of the earth in the short term as much as I can, so I would pay for the expense "maintain your happy place in the short term" regardless of whether I was renting or buying. Cleanliness is next to godliness.

In the medium-term—cut the grass, shovel the sidewalk, paint, and such— the owner pays. In the long-term, if anything big breaks through no fault of anyone except the inevitable decline of stuff turning into junk, the owner is still responsible. New water heater? Leaky roof? Mold problems?

Whenever something big (or even small) has ever broken in my apartments that I've rented, I would just call my landlord, and it would get magically taken care of. If the price to fix whatever just fell apart was more than the landlord anticipated and budgeted, I assume the landlord would consider that when negotiating the new lease terms when the contract expired.

Maintenance for real property can get expensive. What's lurking behind the walls? Were there any improvements that have been made along the way that weren't done correctly? Is there anything that has already far exceeded its life expectancy and will need to be replaced? What necessary updates and renovations will you have to make to ensure it retains its value and doesn't look dated? Owning real property is chock full of unpredictable and annoying costs that you just won't deal with as a renter.

My attempts at minor home improvement projects at my parents' house prove that carpentry is not one of my talents. I'll be a carpenter one day—it's on the Life Bucket List—but right now I'm a petite and weak chica without the tools, physical strength or know-how to fix what's broken, so maintaining the asset would not be cheap for me.

Maybe it's for you. Maybe it's not.

(8) Selling real property is as expensive and (9) complicated to sell as it is to buy. You will likely have to pay a real estate commission for the realtor working on your behalf and a real estate commission for the realtor working on the buyer's behalf. Depending on the negotiation, you'll likely pay for closing costs and certain repairs.

You'll hire a lawyer for the paperwork. You'll vacate your house while it's shown. You'll stage it appropriately and live like super-clean monks for as long as it takes. Your only potential buyers are the pool of people who are looking in that particular area at that particular time. Rough.

(10) Real property is not a fluid way to keep a significant chunk of your net worth. Since selling real property is expensive and complicated, it's not a fluid way to keep your money. If you're not financing from the bank, you're still tying up a significant portion of your funds. Living in the real property and not renting it out means you're not getting dividends in the meantime.

(11) Real property limits your ability to wander and adapt. For all the reasons above, buying real property limits your financial flexibility in a way that buying VTSAX doesn't.

This reason rounds out my top three for why I personally don't plan to buy real property anytime soon. On top of being very expensive and still needing to pay rent, having a good chunk of your personal savings in real property leaves you less able to squeeze life's lemons to make your lemonade.

And life will throw some lemons at you. You just don't know when or where or what variety of lemon. What if climate change picks on your particular neighborhood and batters your house repeatedly with killer floods, tornadoes, hurricanes, earthquakes, sinkholes and killer bees? Maybe your state becomes ground zero for the next Zika. Maybe a major industry collapses and leaves the city desolate and depopulating rapidly. What if you have a crazy, psychotic neighbor? Or you get divorced? What if someone dangles the job of your dreams five thousand miles away?

Dealing with any of those above scenarios becomes a lot harder when a significant portion of your net worth is tied to not just a single country, state, city, neighborhood, block, but one tiny, suffocating plot of land. I'm not saying that you won't be able to squeeze life's lemons, but it will take more squeezing.

In September 2012, I was nearing thirty and had been waiting for the bank to make a decision on the short sale for nearly six months. Frustrated, I hired a home inspector to tell me about the property and what I could expect. I hadn't wanted to pay for this unless it was reasonably certain the deal would go through, but I went ahead for some feeling of progress.

I followed the home inspector around as he pointed things out to me and made notes and took pictures. The back of the condominium had drainage problems. See the tilt in the sidewalk? The air conditioner was not put in correctly. That's a fire hazard. The roof would need to be replaced in a couple of years. There was a significant amount of mold growing in the building that would likely require a large assessment from all the condo owners.

My lawyer suggested asking the sellers to pay the

probable assessment, but the idea of throwing a wrench into the already creaking wheels of this process and asking sellers who were already distressed financially to give me money left me feeling gross. The ominous mold smell and the truly uncertain costs made the decision easy. The bank was still deliberating, and, per the contact, I could still walk away. I paid $400 for the inspector and $300 for the lawyer and *skipped* away.

A year later my firm asked if I wanted to move to Sydney. If I had bought that property, that decision would have been a lot more complicated and stressful.

There's an emotional argument to the idea of owning your own home that I won't discount. I completely understand and empathize with the lure of developing roots in a community, the nesting impulse, stability for your children, the desire to claim a place as your own, to do with what you please, to renovate and paint and customize to your own taste.

If that's your reason to purchase real property—I say, "awesome sauce" to you. Pure sauce. It's an official part of the American Dream, and maybe, if you're lucky, the house will have appreciated when you decide to sell it, and you'll make enough to overcome the expensive hassles.

I personally know several people who have bought their house, lived in it for a decade-plus, loved and tended to it as required, paid the taxes happily as it was less than rent would have been for something similar in their area, sold it for a hefty profit, and moved to another house where they repeat that process. There's no accounting for luck.

But I think I already depend on luck a little too much as it is. I prefer fluidity and flexibility.

CHAPTER 5

How Should I Not Spend My Money?

It's all good to think about saving money in the abstract, but I know you want specific examples of things you should stop buying.

Most things. You can stop buying most things.

Here's something advertisers don't tell you because they're good at their jobs. You don't need many things to be happy, and the odds of the thing they're peddling being the magical purchase that can make you happy is so ridiculous that we're both laughing and simultaneously bonding in our agreement. I told you they're good at their jobs.

You don't need most stuff. You can completely eliminate spending on most of your depreciating assets and decrease the percentage on the rest and be as happy, if not happier, than you currently are.

I know. Telling you to stop buying most stuff is really not helpful advice. So I made a list of things you might want to give up and why. And then I made that list into smaller lists. Because lists are happiness.

Keep in mind that I'm just giving you ideas and my personal pros and cons for each of them. Your calculus might be different. That's the wonderful thing about this. You have almost complete control over how you spend your money. You have the power to make the decisions for yourself. Tired of me telling you this? Let's dive in.

Here are eight things you should not buy because they add negative value to your life.

1. Get-rich-quick schemes
2. Anything to do with a multi-level marketing pitch
3. Timeshares
4. Diamond engagement rings
5. Cigarettes
6. Soda/Pop/Cola
7. Lottery tickets
8. Late fees

Avoid these items and you're already ahead of the curve. These things, in my opinion, only seep energy and money and power from you. You're smart and probably already avoiding all these purchases, so feel free to skip ahead if that's the case.

Get-rich-quick schemes

A fool and his money are soon parted. This is another phrase I didn't make up. If someone comes to you with a new opportunity to MAKE MONEY and is shouting at you like that enthusiastically, I would beware.

I've developed a few rules of thumb for avoiding scams:

- If the salesman is pushy, it's probably because his product stinks. He has to use aggressive sales tactics that confuse and wear people down because his products make no sense.

- If there's time pressure to buy, there's really not.

- When he talks of easy entrepreneurship with the implication that anyone can get rich (and, by extrapolation, it's your fault when you fail to make what he's promising you), he's a jerk.

- If he uses a lot of abbreviations and fancy-sounding made-up words that you don't understand, it's a cult. Cults make up words to distinguish the outsiders.

- If you can't find any negative information on the company online, it's probably a scam. Everyone has detractors. Even me. No negative reviews means either the company is so brand-new that you'll be its first victim (yeah, right). Or, more likely, it uses

- the court system to intimidate and purge negative information about it from the web.
- If you don't understand how you would make money, you're not ready to buy. Read the fine print. Understand the fine print. Be able to explain the fine print in plain English (or whatever your native language). You should always be able to review the information on your own time to make a decision.

I'll give you some specific examples.

Multi-level marketing pitches or pyramid schemes
Multi-level marketing schemes are scams. It's not a way to make money or get rich quickly. It's a way to spend money, prey on friends, baffle me, discourage critical thinking, and waste your precious time and brain juice on something that will only serve to enrich someone who is more entrenched in that particular cult than you are.

I don't really differentiate in my head between the multi-level marketing schemes that the Federal Trade Commission recognizes and the ones that are outright and illegal pyramid schemes. The FTC's website states:

> If the money you make is based on your sales to the public, it may be a legitimate multilevel marketing plan. If the money you make is based on

the number of people you recruit and your sales to them, it's not. It's a pyramid scheme.[10]

Meh. When the only people making a worthwhile hourly wage for their efforts are the ones who are constantly recruiting new members, it's a pyramid scheme. Maybe you have a product to sell to get over the FTC's objections, but the real money comes from growing the cult.

The only way to make a decent hourly wage in pyramid schemes is to be an exceptional salesperson. You need to not only persuade others to purchase your wares; you also need to persuade others to *hawk* your wares.

Oh, and these wares that you're hawking aren't that great. They're wildly overpriced to account for the multiple commissions.

Plus, you'll probably need to buy something to get the business started. Maybe you'll have to buy samples of the product to showcase. Or brochures and bags for the products. Maybe you have to buy seminars and techniques on how to sell the product. Or licenses to sell the product. I don't know. Scammers are constantly thinking of new ways to part you from your money.

Even if you're just peddling your wildly overpriced crap and not persuading others to join you in selling, well, you're *still* peddling your wildly overpriced crap to everyone you meet! It's hard work to drum up new leads and new sales and new souls to throw your parties.

You won't make enough money to justify the work because it's really a lot of work. Some friends will try to support you and maybe they'll buy a thing or two a time or two, but, eventually you're just forcing your friends' financial avatars to knife-fight yours. Don't make them do that.

When you encounter someone who tells you that you're getting in on the ground floor of a great opportunity, picture your financial avatar visiting the pyramids in Egypt. You're on the "ground floor" and the pyramid is burning.

Run! Get out! Now! NOO! Don't arm your financial avatar with a knife and send him to stand at the entrance of the pyramids to lure people into knife fights inside the burning pyramid! Why do I even have to tell you not to do that?!

Is this analogy getting too silly? Well, that's because pyramid schemes are so silly.

I know this is all common sense and I cannot imagine anyone falling for these schemes. But they're ubiquitous, so someone must be falling for them somewhere, right? Maybe we just need to keep hearing shit until we get it. To me, putting stuff on credit cards that you don't need when you don't have the money for it makes as much sense as paying someone money for the right to buy the license to sell the license to sell a water filter.

My Review of The King of Queens, Season 2, Episode 22 – "Soft Touch"

While writing this rant, I watched an old episode of the television show *The King of Queens* that I remembered from years ago. Doug, our titular King of Queens, New York, buys 50 licenses to sell licenses to sell water filters for $1,000 from his neighbor, Tim.

Doug's wife Carrie is skeptical when he tells her of his dealings, but Doug insists that he can make money from this venture and successfully lures his quirky father-in-law, Arthur, to join him. Sadly, Arthur lives in Doug and Carrie's basement, so he can only voice his support and star in hilarious scenes that chronicle his attempts to sell people a license to sell water filters. My personal favorite:

Arthur, talking to some missionaries at the door: "You convert to the Sparkle Tap team and I'll convert to your religion."

That line alone was worth the price of admission. I laughed out loud. My good man, I laughed out loud.

Doug tries to sell these licenses to sell water filters to his friends, Richie and Spencer. Richie, possibly the only character in the show more conventionally "stupid" than Doug, almost bites in this surprisingly candid scene.

Richie and Spencer are drinking glasses of water, while Doug tries to rouse their enthusiasm about the product.
Richie: Alright, I'll take a filter.
Spencer: What the hell, I'll take one too.
Doug: I'm not asking you to just buy a filter. I'm asking you to buy into a way of life.
Richie: I don't even want the filter.

Predictably, nobody wants to buy the license to sell the license to sell water filters and Doug eventually goes over to confront his evil neighbor. Tim, predictably, has already absconded with Doug's money. Absurdity taken to extremes, but still, somehow, effective.

My only complaint is this episode lacks character consistency. Spencer explains to Richie succinctly:

"You have a product with little or no value. The only actual profit comes from constantly recruiting new members which you inevitably run out of. And the whole thing collapses."

I don't think that Spencer would have been that eloquent in casual conversation. This is the same character who will, in a future episode, drive to Vermont to get married so he and his roommate can qualify for a time-share presentation.

Timeshares

Speaking of timeshares. Don't go to a timeshare presentation. I know the sponsor tempts you with free stuff. They have to give you free stuff. Nobody would buy this insanity if there wasn't free stuff to lure you in.

The first time someone tried to sell me on the idea of going to a timeshare presentation, I have to admit that my first thought was "that doesn't sound terrible." The woman on the other end of the line promised me two plane tickets to Las Vegas and two nights in a hotel for only $99 and my attendance at a ninety-minute presentation.

I didn't go because I was only a teenager, but I've since spent an inordinate amount of time cultivating my list—"reasons not to attend a timeshare presentation."

If I were in any sort of debt, I wouldn't go. This $99 "vacation" would still require money for transportation to and from the airport along with food, drink and entertainment expenses for those two days. That money would be better spent towards chipping away at my debt than an impromptu weekend trip.

I could potentially justify that 90 minutes of my life, but as these presentations are notoriously hard to end, I suspect the actual time commitment would end up being closer to a half day. A quarter of my time on that vacation spent pressured into buying something I don't want? Oof, that's a much harder sell.

A half hour of no no no is fine. Four hours plus of no no no no no no no no no no no no no no no no is annoying enough to read; I imagine the experience itself would be a million times worse to live.

Keep in mind that these people need me to cave. If I don't pay, they don't get paid. This is their job and some of them are really, really good at it. They have researched every possible answer and have a counter-answer. They look for your weak spots and poke, poke, poke at you until you have to be rude and yell at them to stop poking you, dammit! You have to demand to leave when 90 minutes is over. You have to feel like a jerk at some point.

I don't enjoy the idea of setting up my financial avatar for a knife fight. Either she gets stabbed or (more likely) she stabs the middleman's financial avatar.

I'm not susceptible to that kind of thing and have faith that I could say no and come out "ahead". But all of us think that, don't we? We all think we drive well. We all think we're smarter than average.

I don't like to tempt the weaknesses in my synapses, so I try to set myself up to succeed. It's better to avoid these kinds of "deals." Even when my financial avatar wins, she's still going to feel rather yucky about the whole interaction.

The pitches for timeshare presentations, like most scams,

are constantly evolving and I think the best response, in the end, is pure avoidance. They'll shout at you in airports offering free or insanely reduced-price experiences or even warm, soft cash if you attend. They'll suggest at the front desk of your hotel. Or maybe they'll call you at your house.

I know they're smiling, but their financial avatars are sharpening their knives. People who sell timeshares have to use aggressive sales tactics that confuse and wear people down because their products make no sense.

Don't go and you win. The teeny tiny minuscule chance that you'll buy into a timeshare company is too scary to contemplate. Not worth the risk, thank you very much.

Buying a timeshare means stabbing your financial avatar in the right hand. A very annoying injury, I would imagine. Even if your financial avatar is left-handed, he won't be able to wash the dishes and will have to live in filth.

A timeshare is an obligation and a burden on your financial avatar (and your financial avatar's heirs!). You're paying a middleman to limit your options. Let me write that again with the urgency it demands. You're *paying* a middleman to *limit* your options. I like to use my money to increase my options and not limit them.

In most cases, you have to give the middleman a down-payment. Oh, if you don't have the cash on hand, he will offer you loans with exorbitant interest rates. No. Just. Gross.

On top of the down payment, you have to pay monthly

maintenance costs. Then when you're ready to use it, you have to pay booking fees or cleaning fees. Gross. If you're suckered into the timeshare industry once, you're officially on their radar. My idea of a nice vacation doesn't involve recurring hassle from someone bugging you to buy more or upgrade.

The people who are happy they bought their timeshare confound me. It sounds like Stockholm Syndrome or locate-the-silver-lining-itis. I love taking vacations. I take a lot of vacations. But the timeshare route to a vacation is probably the most expensive and complicated route one could invent.

With timeshares, you can vacation only at specific places at specific times with advanced planning. It's hard to get out of these timeshare contracts when your life situation changes. People are paying money to give them away.

On eBay, you can find a ton of nice folks willing to pay the $599 closing costs and the resort transfer fee of $250 if you give them $1 and take over the contract and the never-ending maintenance fees. If you're still keen on timeshares, like most things in life, you'll be better off if you buy it used.

I really don't understand the appeal. If you understand the appeal, don't tell me. I'm pretty happy with my opinion.

Diamond engagement rings

I'm not married. I've never been married. I've never even been close to the concept of being married, so maybe I'm not allowed to have an opinion on this. But I have an opinion on this and the more research[11] I did, the more confident my opinion became. Diamond engagement rings are an unnecessary expense and you shouldn't buy them.

Corporations are masters at telling you what you need to feel complete. One of the most successful brainwashers out there is the diamond industry. We like diamonds because they're shiny. A little over a century ago, human beings scooped out only a few diamonds a year from riverbeds. They were rare, and rare means expensive.

But then in 1870, some dudes realized that we could mine diamonds if we dug around in specific spots in the earth. Investors got together to finance the digging and, to their amazement, they found a lot of diamonds. I picture the investors excitedly telling their wives how much money they were set to make off this new venture.

But then a problem occurred. The mines were *too* fruitful and too many diamonds appeared. The more diamonds the world had, the less people were willing to pay for them.

So, the investors all got together, in what I can only assume was in a dark room, with a long table, and evil cackling throughout. The investors decided to control every aspect of the diamond industry, from the mining, to the distribution, to perpetuating the inaccurate perception of their rarity, to their astonishingly successful (and global) advertising campaign equating diamonds, and only diamonds, as the only acceptable token for proposing marriage.

Excellent ad men began to convince people that diamonds equaled love. They insisted that, if a boy was sweet on a girl, he would buy her a diamond ring and surprise her with the gift to signify their love for all eternity. The bigger the better. The more diamonds you squeezed on there, the more you loved her. Diamonds, you see, are forever. Diamonds are symbolic and you can't ever sell or otherwise dispose of them because they are sacred to your emotional bond.

I don't like the idea of a possibly evil cartel with a skewed interest in selling me shit telling me what is sacred to my emotional bond.

Diamonds are supposedly very valuable, right? Okay, try selling your diamond. If you buy gold as an investment (another shiny object we humans get from the ground), you might make some money if you sell it at the right time. But unless you own one of the approximately fifty rarest and finest diamonds in the world however (which I promise you that you don't), your diamond ring is not an investment and will never appreciate in value.

It won't even fetch the same price. Jewelry stores won't buy it back for anywhere close to what you bought it for and individuals won't pay as much for an old diamond ring from some random on the internet. Superstitious folks will scream "bad karma" and back away slowly. The only people making any money off old diamond rings are thieves because even if they sell it for $1, they make a profit.

I think this rant is getting too long, but I can think of more negatives. Consider the possibly horrible conditions of the person (or child) who dug that diamond out for you. Realize that you're signaling to vagabonds that you may have money to steal. And personally, I just finding wearing rings uncomfortable. Using a few months of your working life to buy a diamond ring is a stupid idea.

But I argue both sides because I'm trained as a lawyer or something. Okay, so what's the positive in buying a diamond ring? They're shiny and pretty. I agree that diamonds are shiny and pretty, but you can get them in forms that are not ring-like for much less. And you can get other gems that are shiny if you do prefer ring-like.

The only real reason that I see for buying an expensive diamond engagement ring is because it's easier. You won't feel any social pressure if you simply succumb and buy a big, fat, shiny ring when you propose like you're "supposed to."

Sure, you are most definitely enlightened, and you

completely understand and agree with everything I'm saying. You've read the research I cited and you wish that you could stop this stupid perpetuation, but other people—most importantly the other half of your union—won't understand. It's only a few thousand dollars.

If that's your only reason, buy used. Seriously. You'll get a much better deal that way. Don't be superstitious. Be practical.

Cigarettes

I understand why people like cigarettes. A little smoke break with your pals could be fun, I imagine. And that sweet little nicotine buzz can be so delicious and so satisfying!

At least it's satisfying for a minute.[12] The problem with cigarettes is that the buzz needs to be repeated again and again and again. When you smoke, you fire up the nicotine synapses in your brain. Ugh, those guys are nasty boogers. They're pushy and demanding bullies who will control your life once you let them in.

Cigarettes are full of an addicting combination of ingredients all vying for your undying loyalty while slowly destroying your body. Their distinct, ugly smell lingers on clothes and pets and the elevator long after the interaction ends. Most egregious of all (well, to me since I am a personal finance geek and not a doctor or a veterinarian), this habit can drain hundreds of thousands of dollars from your net worth.

These little rolled up sticks that you light and inhale are not cheap. Cigarettes are an easy commodity for politicians to tax, so the price creeps up insistently. The sin tax, they call it. No, I don't know who they are.

Norm—our friend who likes psychic hotlines—buys everything Mimi doesn't and tells her about it in great detail.

He's a smoker and buys a pack of cigarettes a day. Initially the price of a packet of smokes runs $3 per pack, but the sin tax on it increases an average of 6% per year. Mimi take every cent that Norm spends on these vile things and loans it to Compound Interest Charlie, earning, on average, 7% interest.

After forty years, Norm spent nearly $170,000 on a lifetime of nicotine buzzes. Mimi banked more than $550,000 towards freedom.

In reality, the amount you spend on a lifetime habit of smoking is probably much higher. These figures account only for the actual cost of the cigarettes and the inherent opportunity cost. They don't factor in the cost of use.

Cigarettes are bad for you. They ravage your health. It says so right there on the package! I don't usually make grand, sweeping pronouncements, but I don't waste money on any product that admits it will kill me on the label. That seems like a pretty good rule.

Every individual is different, but if you smoke you

should expect higher medical costs and dental expenses. Your health and life insurance company will also charge you higher premiums.

Most people hate the smell, so you'll see a decrease in resale value from the stink on your possessions. When you sell your car or your home or your clothes, you'll have to accept a discounted price.

If you realize all of these facts and still want to smoke, that little nicotine buzz must be really ferocious.

Pop

Pop. Soda. Coke. Whatever slang you prefer to use for your carbonated, sugary beverage of choice. Caffeine and I do not get along, so this is an easy commodity to avoid for me. I understand the appeal though. Sappy sweetness and addictive caffeine entices most people.

Sadly, sugar can mimic nicotine in its addictiveness and pop has sugar in spades. Soda also plays a major role in the obesity epidemic.[13] Every dentist I know rants about its effects on teeth. Again, great reasons to avoid pop, but if Coca-Cola defied inflation and sold for $0.05/bottle as it did for seventy years, I would despise this commodity less.

The current price of a can of cola varies widely depending on the place of purchase. A bulk purchase of an off brand can be as low as a quarter per can, whereas buying the beverage at a sports stadium can run over $5.

Norm likes Dr. Pepper and spends an average of $2/day in the first year he discovers it. Through inflation and increased consumption, the amount he spends creeps up an average of 3% per year. Mimi take the money Norm spends on soda and invests it in a fund earning, on average, 7% per year.

After forty years, Norm spent more than $55,000 on a lifetime of empty calories. Mimi banked another $228,000.

Again, that's the cost of just the soda itself. If you're drinking that much sugar, you're probably in for higher medical costs. My dentist friends will benefit especially, as you'll need to spend more to fix your teeth. They're good people though, so they're not excited about it.

Lottery tickets

Yes, of course, I understand the upside of playing the lottery. If you don't play, you can't win. In one day, with the right guess, you could solve all your problems and all of your friend's problems and all of your neighbor's problems. Money solves everything. Large volumes of money solves large volumes of everything.

I will concede that there is a slight, tiny, miniscule chance that the dice could roll in your favor and you'll win the jackpot. But if you don't already have a healthy relationship with money, there's a better than even chance that you'll blow it all and end up less happy than when you started.[14] Money actually doesn't solve everything.

But, in reality, you won't win. I'm not going to tell you all the many things that have a better chance of happening, because it's all so cliché. But just know that you will not win. I view buying lottery tickets as essentially paying for delayed disappointment.

I bought a bunch of scratch-off lottery tickets for a Christmas present one December. The tickets cost me $30, and the recipient won $21. Not a great return on investment. The government counts on this fact. They wouldn't sell tickets if they thought they were going to lose money off them. Everything is carefully calculated, and the odds are not ever in your favor.

Some of these scratch-off tickets can cost up to $30 *each*! Surely, there are better ways to spend your money.

Norm doesn't buy lottery tickets, so I'm not going to calculate the savings. You get the point, though.

Late fees

I can't think of any upsides for paying late fees. Can you?

You have your wiggle room, right? That means you have the money in the bank to pay on time. Waiting to pay it makes no sense to me. You know you owe the money to a utility company, credit card company, etc. Why pay more by paying late?

Laziness perhaps? It takes only a few minutes, and I love the feeling of accomplishment when I cross off "pay such and such bill."

Whenever I would move, I would launch *Operation No Late Fee*. I made sure all my recurring bills were set for automatic payment. The company will email you when the bill is due, giving you a heads up on how much you owe and when he plans to stop by and grab it off your financial avatar's dresser. You'll never be late. Easy peasy, lemon squeezy.

These are more things that I don't spend money on, but unlike the first list, I won't silently judge you for indulging in these.

1. Cable
2. Coffee
3. Meat
4. Manicures/pedicures
5. Cars
6. Pets

I can already sense your criticisms of this particular list. Curbing the latte habit is such a cliché in personal finance. Very true. Cable probably won't be around in forty years, and the costs are uncertain. Yup. I'm insane, and you're not giving up meat. I know.

My bigger point with this list is to think about the purchase before you spend money on it. I'm just giving you examples. Get your brains churning. In a good way.

Cable

I see the value of cable. Maybe television is your primary form of entertainment. If that's the case and you don't spend much money or time going out or doing anything else, you can probably persuade me it's worth the cost for you.

My parents watch a lot of CNN, and I don't criticize them. If you're a sports buff and have no other way of catching the game, paying for cable is likely cheaper than going to every game. Shutting off your brain at the end of the night with some passive entertainment is an indulgence I cannot fault.

I don't pay for cable because I spent too much time watching it when I did. I also liked cutting down my brain's access to advertisements and thus its ability to create wants. Plus, I can't imagine that watching the number of hours a day I used to watch television exactly enriched my life.

Initially, however, my main motivator was the potential savings from ditching cable.

Norm, of course, loves cable and pays $61.63/month for his viewing habit, a price that creeps up an average of

4.8% per year.*[15] Mimi takes the money Norm spends on cable and puts it in the fabulous 7% fund.

After forty years, Norm spent more than $85,000 on his television-watching habit. Mimi took the $85,000 and turned it into more than $300,000 by loaning it to CI Charlie.

That number doesn't include the decrease in electricity from not using a cable box. If you try shutting off your cable box for *Operation Lower Your Electric Bill*, I bet you'll notice a stark difference. Those things use a lot of power.

Coffee

I don't like caffeine and caffeine assures me the feeling is mutual, so coffee is another easy commodity for me to avoid. I'm pretty sure everybody else disagrees and drinks copious amounts of it.

I suspect that most people primarily enjoy the taste—the warm, bitter, disgusting taste. Maybe there are health benefits. Maybe not. Coffee is similar to pop in terms of cost, but I concede that coffee is not as unequivocally terrible.

The current price of a cup of coffee varies widely depending on the place of purchase and the type of coffee. Making a plain cup of black coffee at home can cost as little

---

* Actually the average American paid much more for basic cable in 2012. That number excludes taxes, fees, and equipment charges.

as a few pennies, whereas buying a fancy sounding drink at a coffee shop can run over $5.

Norm makes terrible decisions. After every soda he guzzles, he then sips a cup of coffee. He spends an average of $2/day. Through inflation and increased consumption, the amount he spends creeps up an average of 3% per year. Mimi takes the money Norm spends on coffee and invests it in a fund earning, on average, 7% per year.

After forty years, Norm spent more than $55,000 on coffee to stay awake. Mimi banked another $228,000 for retirement and took naps. Glorious naps.

Manicures/pedicures

I've had my toenails painted at a salon in the past. I absolutely understand why people like to get this vanity done. It's fun! You feel pampered during the process and oh-so-pretty afterward.

Unfortunately, the polish never seems to last for more than a few days before it's an ugly, chippy mess that I feel compelled to pick at. Plus, as my chemical engineer father always used to remind me as a child, nail polish is a carcinogen. The UV-curing step in salons can also cause cancer.

Adding in the possibility of nail fungus and the probability of nail damage, the appeal greatly lessens for me. I've also read that some nail salons take horrible advantage of their employees.

The final bullet point for me though is the money. Fancy nails can easily set you back $30 and perhaps even triple that for fake nails, nail art, gel, studs, and accessories. Those costs quickly add up.

Meat

Before you dismiss me, let me say that I do understand that food is a highly personal choice, and I have no right to tell you what you can or cannot put into your mouth. I realize this will be a very hard sell for most of you reading this. Okay, that's cool. I'm not judging. My parents raised me vegetarian, so I've never missed meat. For me personally, not buying meat is a no-brainer.

The environmental effect of factory farming animals is breathtaking for its breadth—from the methane that contributes to climate change, waste runoff into the waterways, deforestation for growing cattle herds, to the consumption of resources used for feed, to name a scant few.

My biggest qualm is the truly horrific life that each factory-farmed animal is forced to endure before he dies and gets to the kitchen. If slaughtering billions of creatures who know only fear and pain and suffering for most of their time on this earth isn't wrong, then *nothing* is wrong.

Okay, maybe I am silently judging you.

But meat, I'm told, is delicious. End of argument.

From a financial standpoint, though, it's worth remembering that meat is often the most expensive part of a meal. The vast majority of time, the vegetarian items on the menu are the cheapest. Saving money is pretty far down the list of reasons of why I don't eat meat, but the costs add up quickly. Notice the price of the vegetarian items in restaurants. Calculate the cost of subtracting all meat from your grocery receipt, and you'll see what I'm talking about.

Even if you can't go completely meatless, try doing it one day a week. Or one meal a day. Or one lifetime of your many lifetimes. My vote is this lifetime!

Pets

Put down your pitchforks, people! I love pets. I will most certainly have at least a cat and probably a dog when (if?) I settle down in one place again.

Whenever I visit my parents and remember our family cat Daisy that passed away years ago, I subtly try to persuade them to adopt a new cat by telling them they should get a cat. I make a beeline to a pet when I see one at other people's houses. I had a foster cat that I adored when I lived in Chicago. Pet-sitting is one of life's joys.

But as much as it pains me to type this, pets are a want and not a need.

If you're reading this while sitting next to Megatron— your adorable fluffy cat that you've had since she was a tiny kitten and that name was hilarious—you're going to think I'm crazy and cruel. She's been with you through so many of your heartaches and so many of your joys, and she is a member of your family and you love her more than you love me.

I know. You're not going to get rid of her. Debt be damned.

The pros of pets are easy to come up with and why you probably already have one. There are likely health benefits such as lower stress and possibly longer life expectancy, companionship, exercise if you walk the dog daily, unconditional love, a snuggle buddy, a babe magnet, a conversation starter, and happiness.

I'm just saying—they're expensive, yo. The initial acquisition cost, food, health care, toys, grooming, housing, boarding for when you're on vacation, doggie daycare, and whatever else they persuade you to buy, quickly add up. The costs are also unpredictable if Megatron gets sick.

So please, calculate and consider the ongoing costs of getting a pet before you go out and fall in love with her. Sentiment and emotions make us human. I like to think that the ability to plan and consider everything also makes us human.

You really have to think hard if they are worth the money you spend on them. It's probably better to ponder this thought and make a decision before you invite them into your home, because they will be nearly impossible to give up once acquired. Damn you, feelings and emotions!

If you've thought about it and really are ready and able and willing to take on responsibility for another creature, don't pay an insane amount for a purebred animal. Shelter pets are much cheaper and will be forever grateful for your choice.

Cars

Cars! Woot, right? Cars are powerful, convenient, warm in the winter, cool in the summer, gloriously lacking in strangers, shiny status symbols. Not owning a car is almost un-American, eschewing all that she has to offer—the wide-open country, the spacious suburbs, the quintessential road trip. For a new driver, a car means freedom.

On the other hand, cars are responsible for about a quarter of carbon dioxide emissions. Their appetite for gasoline contributes to questionable regimes abroad, and motor vehicle incidents are the fifth leading cause of death.

All good reasons for and against car ownership, but the tipping point for me came after calculating how much this habit cost me. For most of us, cars are probably the most expensive depreciating asset we buy.

I've never technically owned a car. During my teenage driving years, I used my parents' cars. When I graduated college and worked in insurance, I used a family car. My father put the down payment on it (about $7,000), my mother and sister held the title on it, and I made the monthly payments on it until it was paid off three years later.

I spent an obscene amount of time driving for my insurance job and a tolerable amount during law school. It was my faithful friend for six years, but upon graduation, I abandoned that beauty in my parent's driveway and never looked back.

In my strategy to eliminate my student loans as quickly as possible, kicking my car to the curb greatly improved my financial situation. With this one move, I simplified my budget, eliminating a ridiculous number of categories for money to slip through, such as:

1. Cost of the car/depreciation of the car
2. Gasoline
3. Maintenance
4. Parking
5. Vandalism
6. Tickets
7. Accidents
8. Repairs
9. Car insurance
10. Savings for next car or interest on car loan

Phew! With all of these expenses, I tend to think of cars as a liability and not an asset. Let's say Norm buys a new car for $13,000 every ten years. Mimi prefers to bike, so she buys her investment fund, earning 7% per year in interest.

After forty years, Norm has spent $52,000 on cars. Mimi took that money and turned it into almost $370,000. These numbers take into account only the very first category of car ownership—the cost of the car. Norm doesn't actually drive the car. Instead, he keeps it in his driveway to annoy the neighbors.

If Norm actually wanted to use the car, Mimi would leap into the air with excitement. For simplicity sake, let's say he spends $1,000 a year on gasoline, maintenance, insurance, parking, tickets, repairs, etc. Mimi takes that money (hence the leap with excitement) and throws it into her wonderful investment.

After forty years, Norm spent an additional $40,000 and has an extra ten pounds around his mid-section to show for it. Mimi prefers her lower resting heart rate and nearly $600,000.

You can spend much, much more than $13,000 on a car. We both know that. These calculations also assume that Norm doesn't finance the car and has enough money on hand to pay for it outright.

Purely in terms of personal finance and budgeting, cars are one of the worst items to buy. The various expenses involved are many, large, fixed, variable, often completely out of your control, and hard to understand if you're not a mechanic.

If you must own a car, at least know the numbers and understand thrifty ways to lessen the impact on your net worth. For instance, wait as long as you can between car purchases. Buy a slightly used car. See if you can get by with only one car. Obvious advice, no?

Consider this well-known factoid. As soon as you drive a new car off the lot, the value of your new "asset" drops 11%. 11%! When the stock market drops 11%, the cable news networks do not shut up about it. They call it a correction and calculate how much money the world collectively lost.

But every 2.6 seconds, some sucker takes his hard-earned money and buys what is often the most (or second-most) expensive asset he will ever buy. The minute this sucker drives it off the lot, it loses 11% of its value that it will never recover. No cable news story about this, though.

I'm not judging you if you do have a car. Some places just don't make it possible to bike or walk or use public transportation to get everywhere.

But a lot of places do make it possible to bike or walk or use public transportation. You just kind of forget that fact because you have your car.

I hope I didn't alienate you complaining about all the things you might have spent your money on. I like to think I give both sides of the argument for each item, but for me and my lifestyle, the answer is obvious to avoid them.

You can find something wrong with every single purchase if you look hard enough. Depriving yourself of everything is also not the right way to live.

Buy what actually brings you happiness. When you do find something worthy of your almighty dollar, enjoy the item! I've started thanking my things after I use them. Gratitude is the seed of happiness. Appreciate all the universe has loaned you.

Your attitude is the part you can control. You can believe that stuff is evil, destroying our planet, making us miserable, and draining our wallets. Or you can believe that stuff is good, helping you on your journey through life. If you're picky about what you let into your life and only allow in things that spark joy, it's a lot easier to brandish the right attitude.

And so you don't think I live in a cave eating berries, wearing nothing but a loincloth, I'm sharing my list of things I spend money on. If you don't spend money on these items, you can feel a smudge superior.

Seven things I purchase, with varying frequency

1. Books
2. Music

3. Movies
4. Travel
5. Eating in restaurants
6. Alcohol
7. Eyebrow threading

Books

So far I have tried to flesh out the arguments for and against each spending habit draining your net worth, but in the case of books, I have nothing but glowing things to say about them. Books are one of my primary sources of entertainment and my favorite hobby. I love books.

Books can drain your net worth if you let them, but I seldom find it necessary. I pay Mayor Civil before I even pay myself, and he buys a lot of books. I mean, every book you can think of. And he lets me borrow them! He even set it up so I can request whatever book I want online. When it's ready, he emails me! It's usually only a few days later.

I'm talking, of course, about the magical place called the library.

I do occasionally purchase books. If the library has already lent out all of the copies of the book I need to read in time for my next book club meeting or if I find a book that really resonates with me that I want to keep, I will happily buy it.

Norm and Mimi are both voracious readers. The

library fills most of Mimi's reading desires, whereas Norm loves wandering through bookstores, picking up shiny new hardcovers and filling his Kindle with every novel that seems remotely interesting.

Mimi spends $50/year on books while Norm spends $1,000. Mimi takes the difference ($950/year) and invests it in VTSAX with Compound Interest Charlie, earning her an average of 7% per year.

After forty years, Norm has an impressive personal library, most of which is stored in boxes in his basement, as he ran out of bookshelves long ago. Mimi has more than $200,000. And just for kicks, I'll throw in Dude. He hates to read and invested the whole $1,000/year. He now has almost $214,000, but his life makes me sad.

Music

I like music I can sing along to, but I do not possess an ounce of musical aptitude, so the radio (now internet radio) meets all of my needs. I realize that I am probably in the minority here, though.

Maybe music is your profession or your passion. Maybe you live for concerts, and buying a new album every week makes you thrive. You will hear no complaint from me if you attend concerts, but spending money on a physical music collection just seems like a waste of money and space while taunting the technology gods. Remember cassette tapes?

Mimi spends $50/year on her music habit, mostly on concerts, while Norm spends $1,000/year enhancing his media collection. He wants his music selection to rival his book and movie selection, so he buys a new vinyl record or CD every couple of weeks. Mimi invested the difference ($950/year) and has another $200,000 to show for it after forty years.

Remember, even if you don't want to cut a habit out of your life completely, moderating the habit and indulging in it smartly can shave years off your working life. Frequency matters, because you'll never get rich spending your money on depreciating assets.

Movies

I don't see much wrong with movies either, but my attention span responds better to television shows. I may go to the movies when a friend asks, if (1) the movie is based on a book and (2) it's a book I've read. Even then, I may say no. Movie theaters are really cold.

The cost of watching a movie depends very much on how you watch it. A 3-D movie in an IMAX theater with snacks and drinks can easily run over $50, while renting one from a vending machine in the grocery store can set you back a whole dollar or two. A movie collection of

DVDs (or Blu-ray or VHS cassettes or whatever the latest obsolete technology is) can steal thousands from your net worth and clutter your shelves.

Mimi spends $50/year on her movie habit, while Norm spends $1,000/year seeing movies in the theater and purchasing a new DVD every couple of weeks. Mimi invests the difference as in the previous example. After forty years, she can't declare herself a movie buff, but she does have another $200,000 that Norm does not.

Books, music, and movies are things I spend money on approximately two to three times per year, but if I bumped that number up to one to two times per week, I might consider the habit a drain. Frequency matters on all things consumption!

Travel

Now we're getting to the heart of my spending. I spend most of my cash traveling on airplanes and boats and trains and buses and occasionally a car that isn't mine (e.g. cabs). In that budget bucket I also put in accommodations I use while visiting new places.

Mentally, I mean. I don't keep budget buckets.

My obsession with crossing stuff off lists extends to my "visited countries list." I love seeing a new city and wandering around it. Look at what exists! Look at what mankind has built! Oh, nature made that! Even better!

Consequently, I spend a *lot* of money on flights and temporary accommodations. Even with frequent flier miles and scouring the internet for deals, this is still my largest expense, by far.

And it most definitely adds up. This habit is also terrible for Mother Earth, spewing fumes in the air and producing contrails. You could argue it's also a waste of my life and my time. I'd disagree with you, but you could probably make a compelling argument.

One might even suggest that my transient lifestyle fosters a lot of friendships, but not *close* friendships. The research on happiness shows that *close* friendships boost happiness, not just friendships. I don't have all of life figured out yet, so I may agree with you on this one day.

And I know that "traveling the world" is a dream a lot of people have. If that's your dream too, it doesn't have to be expensive. If you have time, you can travel slowly. Buy one-way tickets and leisurely hang out in a place for a bit. Renting an apartment for a month costs much less per day than a hotel for five days.

There are hostels and low-cost countries. You can couch-surf or house-sit. Make friends when you travel, and visit them. Play the credit card game for free miles. The possibilities are endless.

Restaurants

I'm learning to cook whenever I visit my mom because "learn to cook like Mom" is on the Life Bucket List. I can't take that off.

But, honestly, I hate cooking. I'd much rather have a banana and call it a day than dirty and then wash all those dishes. Some people even take the time to dry the dishes afterward with a towel. Crazy.

I eat out quite a bit since a banana isn't enough sustenance. I'm a single gal, so making big meals for myself doesn't feel like the best use of my time. I also view eating out with friends and drinking as my major social activity.

I know this habit puts a severe strain on my net worth. Cooking at home is so much cheaper.

I'm still learning.

Alcohol

One day, I'll be a teetotaler and give up drinking. But right now, I quite enjoy the taste of alcohol. I love a good craft beer, red wine, mixed drink that is an unnatural blue color with a funky umbrella sticking out of it.

Drinking and eating out with friends is my main social activity. I may have mentioned that already. I love raising my glass and "cheers-ing" to something ludicrous and trying spirits in different countries. I love lowering my inhibitions and making friends over booze. Even when I was trying to pay off my student loans, going out drinking with friends was never something I gave up. I participated less than I do now, but I still drank.

And I know this habit drains my net worth. A lot! Liquor is expensive. It can easily add up to cost more than the meal in a restaurant. Buy enough shots and your credit card will shudder. Top-shelf moonshine can run into the triple digits. Throw a sparkler into a bucket with ice and the bottle and have it delivered to you by a pretty girl, and you can expect to spend hundreds of dollars for this table service. Pricey!

The studies aren't completely sure, but alcohol is probably bad for the body, too. At the very least, excessive alcohol is bad for you. Ever hear of beer belly? That's caused by the calories from beer. Drink too much too often, and your stomach will turn into a belly. Jiggly.

Finally, and probably most importantly, people make stupid decisions when they're drunk. They can be loud and aggravating. Or annoying. They can declare their love for everyone and everything. Obnoxiously.

I'm pretty sure it's all about moderation.

Eyebrow threading

This is a small thing, but so are many of the items I complained about you buying. I get my eyebrows threaded by a professional every few weeks because I'm of Indian descent and a rather hairy creature.

Theoretically, I could pluck my eyebrows myself, but I can't get the polished look of threading with tweezers. I could also learn to thread my own eyebrows. But I haven't. And I have no plans to, because I like burning money.

No, seriously. I tell you this because I know we all have our vices. We all spend our money on things that give us pleasure. That's what money is for. That's the point of it all!

All I'm asking is that you consider everything before you buy, and make sure you really want the thing you want and that it's not some clever advertising messing with your brain and your wallet. Nobody cares about your money as much as you do. Look at the item you want to buy, and ask yourself if it brings you more joy than having more free time.

Most things won't. But some things will. Only you can decide what those things are.

One thing I used to purchase, but don't anymore
1. Earrings

I love earrings. I have three earring holes in my left ear and two earring holes in my right ear. Picking out which earrings to wear in the morning is one of life's joys. Dangly, pretty, colorful, tasteful, shiny baubles. The thrill of crossing off the "buy a pair of earrings" travel bucket list item is so easily obtained!

But I realized eventually that the sadness from my earring selection outweighed the joy. I have too many and don't even notice when I've lost a favorite pair until my mom asks about them.

A good percentage of my earring collection can claim souvenir status, but at this point, I don't remember which country exactly each came from. There are even a few pathetic earrings that live in a box, never going near my earlobe, collecting dust at one of my frequent pit stops.

Doesn't that seem kind of sad to you, too?

When you have a lot of one thing, you tend to value it less and treat what you do have poorly. You start to think of it as dispensable. Because it is dispensable to you. You can't keep track of all that shit. That's the pitfall of abundance. If you have too much, it's hard to appreciate what you have. The more you accumulate, the less it all individually means.

I'm still learning, but that one I've learned.

CHAPTER 6
Still Skeptical?

STILL SKEPTICAL? I understand. There are a lot of things I didn't address, because I don't feel qualified to discuss them. Like children. I don't have kids, so I feel asinine giving you advice on yours. I do have a game plan if my life path one day includes raising a human being, though.

Babies don't need much, if any, new stuff. Used baby stuff is everywhere. Everywhere. Cloth diapers, homemade baby food, breastfeeding are all ways to keep expenses down. The most expensive part of raising children is childcare. I'm retired, so I could stay home with my theoretical babies. If you have control over your time, you could, too. Plus, spending time with your child creates the precious relationship bond we already talked about.

I wouldn't find it necessary to save up and pay for my nonexistent child's college either. I'd hope that I raised

STILL SKEPTICAL?

them to be intelligent enough to find their own way. I had student loan debt and, yes, it sucked. For sure. But it also helped me understand money a bit more and the value of my time.

I also didn't really talk about health insurance. We live in a society where health care is not a fundamental human right, and the sad reality is that you can go bankrupt from an unfortunate health incident even if you're employed. The idea of staying in a job you hate just for access to health insurance makes me want to cry. If you get sick, you can fly to another country for cheaper treatment. You can call around to see if paying cash would get you a better deal. I know this is not a very satisfying answer.

At the end of the day, you have to plan your own life and tailor it to your available resources and circumstances. Just keep all your options on the table, and you'll see how much possibility the universe has granted you.

My dad was skeptical of my retirement plans as well. Here's a letter I wrote to him six months after I retired.

> Dear Dad,
>
> I've been officially "retired" for just over six months now and you still occasionally ask me if I have any income, if I plan to ever work as a lawyer again, if I have health insurance. I explain to you my numbers and my charts and that seems to appease you for the

minute, but I can sense that you're worried. And bewildered. I went to law school. I'm supposed to be a lawyer. That's how these things work.

I'm going to be fine. Please don't worry about me and my finances because I'm not worried about me and my finances. That previous sentence may possibly be my single greatest achievement in life to date. Except, of course, the time I ate three grilled cheese sandwiches in one sitting. What a glorious day that was.

But money? Money doesn't even grace the top ten list of my worries. Yes, of course I have a list of my current worries. I find that if I write things down, they take up less space in my brain. Here is an excerpt of one of my least favorite lists—"My Worry List."

Anita's 2016 Worry List
1. Climate change
2. Judge Judy retiring
3. Antibiotics obsolescence
4. Horse-race politics
5. Lieutenant Benson drinking too much on *Law & Order: SVU*
6. The Golden State Warriors beating the '95-'96 Bulls' single-season win record

7. The realization that I still haven't filed my 2015 taxes
8. The yellow spots on my eyes
9. Dying alone
10. The epidemic of gun violence in the United States and our apparent inability to address it

In contrast, here is an excerpt of My Worry List when I started working in 2010.

Anita's 2010 Worry List
1. My student loans
2. My law firm realizing I'm a fraud and that they made a horrible mistake in hiring me
3. My negative net worth
4. The realization that I hate being a lawyer
5. Not being able to travel
6. Work taking away all my free time
7. Climate change
8. Horse race politics
9. The epidemic of gun violence in the United States and our apparent inability to address it
10. Dying alone

Sometime in the past six years, I stopped worrying about money. I'm not sure when it was exactly, but gradually, as various items fell off my

Worry List, my ball of anxiety surrounding money got smaller and smaller.

I paid off my last student loan. I accumulated my first $100,000. Investing started to make sense to me. Milestones passed. I hit my minimum number for retirement. One day I started writing my Worry List and I realized that nothing about my finances made the cut. **The most valuable thing money can buy is freedom from worrying about money.** Money can't make you happy, but the lack of money can certainly make you unhappy. Maybe I should bold the second sentence because I bold that first one a lot.

I know my stash certainly helped kill the anxiety money monster inside me, but I think it's also my attitude. Let's say I drain all my liquid accounts and all my investment accounts and all my retirement accounts are wiped out by a particularly vicious stroke of rotten luck.

Well, that blows.

On the bright side, I still have my legal degree. And the ability to work in a coffee shop. I could go back to various articles on my blog and figure out how to be an "affiliate" and make money off clicks. More importantly, I know how to thrive and be happy with what most people would consider a small amount of money. I also have my brain, which I'm quite fond of.

Right. And the odds of me losing my entire nest egg are comfortingly small. In fact, the odds are decent that I won't ever have to earn money again, period. I didn't dive into this early retirement blind. I've been tracking my expenses for years. I've read more investment books than I can count.

So, Male Parental Unit, please don't worry about me. I've had an easy life because you've had such a hard life. After moving to Australia, I started to understand, to a fraction of a percent, how difficult it was for you to come to the United States from India for college, so far away from everyone you knew and loved, speaking a different language and trying to make something of yourself.

You tell me tales of sleeping on newspapers in your empty apartment, going hungry waiting for the next check from your family, the racism that you encountered, the years as a dishwasher in a restaurant. You eventually built a career as a chemical engineer and now you own your home, your cars, and live comfortably in retirement, but I wonder how much of your money anxiety remains.

I know that mom doesn't share the same worry about my working situation. I know because she tells me. Repeatedly. Now that I have all my professional and monetary issues sorted, she really thinks I should try harder on the relationship front and that "dying alone" should rank higher on my Worry List. I'll get on that.

Dad, thank you for working so hard so that your children could have an easier life. I owe my success to you and I'm so lucky to have such a good father. I started my blog as a way to keep my anxiety in check and I hope that it assuages yours as well.

Love,

Anita (your youngest and favorite daughter)

Each day consists of only two strolls around the clock and no more. You can do *anything* you want, but you can't do *everything* you want. Opportunity costs exist. We have only a blink of time. One blink.

We live in the most advanced and best time in the history of humanity, with so much freedom and opportunity. How do you want to spend your blink? Money is one tiny part of life that can be either an incredible advantage or a crushing obligation. Don't take the path of least resistance. Try a bunch of different paths to see which view you like the best. Chase the bigger dream. Choose the bigger life.

Now that I'm retired, my world rocks even more than I

thought possible. Money lets me dictate my own schedule. I don't buy things, but I buy my time and do what I want with my days. I sleep when I'm tired and wake up when I'm not. This might be my favorite thing about my life. It's such a luxury. I love sleeping.

My waking hours are fun too, of course. I found the thing I want to do repeatedly—writing. I write for two hours most days, occasionally much less and sometimes much more. I'm constantly reading books.

I hang out with my friends. I talk to my family. Long, leisurely walks are my specialty. I make travel plans and look forward to the next whatever. You'll often find me gazing at my Life Bucket List and plotting. I laugh and smile a lot. I *feel* genuinely happy.

It's the journey, and the journey has some incredible views. As I'm writing this, I'm realizing it's Sunday night. I had to look the day up. I'm doing what I love (writing), and it doesn't feel like work. The days of the week have lost their power over me. I'm no longer living for the weekends.

I love my life because I feel like I am in control of it. I feel free. That's enough.

LIST OF LISTS

I make a lot of lists. Here are a few of them.

Things you need to be happy
    I. Necessary, but not sufficient
        A. A happy place to lay your head at night
        B. Easy access to good, healthy food
        C. Your health
        D. Any one of II, III, or IV below
    II. Pleasant interactions (good relationships)
        A. Supportive family
        B. Close friends
        C. Inner ally
    III. Feeling of control
    IV. Sense of purpose and progress

My broad general rules for spending (with many caveats and exceptions)
    1. Buy security.

2. Don't buy crap.
3. Prioritize spending on experiences and making memories.
4. Spend money on building and maintaining relationships.
5. Thoughtful spending on what you really do is okay.
6. Buy the power of compounding interest.
7. Buy your time.

That's all.

(I think.)

Components of Security
1. A happy place to lay your head at night
2. Enough good, nutritious food to eat consistently and without worry
3. Your health
4. The ability to squeeze life's lemons

How good credit and financial literacy make life easier and better and cheaper and happier
1. Better interest rates on credit cards
2. Better interest rates for mortgages
3. Landlords prefer renters with good credit
4. Employers prefer employees with good credit
5. Payday loan shops with exorbitant, predatory interest rates aren't needed, ever

6. Never pay check-cashing fees
7. Or other bank fees
8. Or late fees because you don't have the money
9. Rent-to-own stores are also never utilized
10. Never pay interest (for the harder core)
11. Pawn shops are only a curiosity
12. Save money on shoes

How to be successful (happy) in life and components of grit

1. Find something you like to do.
2. Make that thing the thing you repeatedly do.
3. Keep doing it. Get better at it. Get up after you fall down and keep going. This is basically the same point as the second point, but important enough that I'm listing it twice.
4. Always believe that you have some control over doing better at that thing tomorrow.
5. Believe what you're doing matters to other people.

Things to keep in mind to avoid being parted with your money

1. If the salesman is pushy, it's probably because his product stinks. Salespeople have to use aggressive sales tactics that confuse and wear people down because their products make no sense.

2. If there's time pressure to buy, there's really not.
3. When there's talk of easy entrepreneurship with the implication that anyone can get rich (and, by extrapolation, it's your fault when you fail to make what he's promising you), he's a jerk.
4. If he uses a lot of abbreviations and fancy-sounding made-up words that you don't understand, it's a cult. Cults make up words to distinguish the outsiders.
5. If you can't find any negative information on the company online, it's probably a scam. Everyone has detractors. Even me. No negative reviews means either the company is so brand new that you'll be their first victim (yeah, right). Or, more likely, they use the court system to intimidate and purge negative information about them from the internet.
6. If you don't understand how you would make money, you're not ready to buy. Read the fine print. Understand the fine print. Be able to explain the fine print in plain English (or whatever your native language). You should always be able to review the information on your own time to make a decision.

How to Get Over Someone

1. Write a list of things you dislike about that person.
2. Throw away your list of things you love about that

person. (You'll regret number two in a few years, but it'll help now. And now is more important than a few years from now. At least for these purposes.)
3. Go out and do things. All the things.
4. Yoga. Lots of yoga and Pilates. Look as good as you want to feel.
5. Flirt. Smile at that guy over there. I bet he'll come over and talk to you.
6. Cry. Mourn.
7. Go to therapy to work on your bigger life problems.
8. Put "*be over whatshisface*" on your "Someday list," and cross it off triumphantly when you're ready.
9. Write a future email to yourself asking if you're over him yet. Send it far enough into the future where you know the answer will be unequivocally yes.
10. Throw self off cliff; start life anew as a penguin. Or a tomato. I would make such a kick-ass tomato.

Disclaimer: Taking relationship advice from me is a really terrible idea.

Conditions that are crucial to making close friends
1. Proximity
2. Repeated, unplanned interactions
3. Setting that encourages people to let their guard down and confide in each other

Operation Enjoy Rules
1. Plan something fun to do every day.
2. The "something" must be outside your apartment if you're by yourself.

List of questions to ask yourself about each item on your Wants List
1. Is this an item that I know to be useful or believe to be beautiful?
2. Will buying this item make my life better or worse in the long run?
3. What is the opportunity cost of using that money instead of buying more VTSAX?
4. What are the externalities of that item?
   a. What are the environmental implications for the production and distribution of this product?
   b. What were the conditions for the person making this item?
   c. What will happen to that item once it is no longer useful or beautiful?
   d. Does buying this item help someone else greatly?

ACKNOWLEDGMENTS

My people

Sheila Dhake, my eldest sister and the only person who reads everything before I let it out into the world. I couldn't do this without you to parse the profoundness.

Katie List, my first editor and my longest and best friendship. I relish the wisdom bomb that I know is coming when I see an email from you in my inbox.

Carol Longhenry, my high school English teacher. So many of your comments on my teenage papers stuck in my brain and shout at me when I'm editing. The shouting makes my writing better. Thank you for beta reading.

Richard Nelson and Reshma Dhake, a couple of members of my first book club, the Greedy Readers. Thank you for being greedy readers and for beta reading.

Dan Swanton, the first person I met who understood my retirement plan, because he had the same plan. Thank you for beta reading.

Dan Crissman, my professional editor who murdered my precious words and made this book so much better than what it was.

Judge Judy. I love watching you call people out on their ridiculousness. Thank you for being so badass. I know you have no idea who I am.

Gail vaz Oxlade. I remember the first time I watched your show, *Til Debt Do Us Part,* and you told people their spending habits were crazy. What a fun job you have.

And you! Thank you for reading my book. It's for you!

Illustrations by Luis Muñiz
Cover design by Damonza.com

BOOKS YOU SHOULD READ

Your Money or Your Life: Transforming Your Relationship with Money and Achieving Financial Independence (1993) by Joe Dominguez and Vicki Robins, for an excellent way to craft your attitude towards money.

The Happiness Project: Or, Why I Spent a Year Trying to Sing in the Morning, Clean My Closets, Fight Right, Read Aristotle, and Generally Have More Fun (2009) by Gretchen Rubin, for creating habits that lead to happiness.

Grit: The Power of Passion and Perseverance (2016) by Angela Duckworth, for motivation and a road-map to success.

The Life-Changing Magic of Tidying Up (2014) by Marie Kondo for jump-starting your stuff purge.

REFERENCES

1. Kristin Neff, *Self Compassion: The Proven Power of Being Kind to Yourself* (Harper Collins, 2011).

2. Judy Sheindlin, *What Would Judy Say: Be the Hero of Your Own Story* (2014), accessed July 31, 2017, http://www.whatwouldjudysay.com/be-the-hero.

3. Alex Williams, "Friends of a Certain Age Why Is It Hard To Make Friends Over 30?" *New York Times*, July 13, 2012.

4. "The Beauty of Life," a lecture from the Birmingham Society of Arts and School of Design (February 19, 1880), later published in *Hopes and Fears for Art: Five Lectures Delivered in Birmingham, London and Nottingham, 1878-1881* (1882).

5. Barry Commoner, "Frail Reeds in a Harsh World," New York: The American Museum of Natural History. Natural History. Journal of the American Museum of

Natural History, Vol. LXXVIII No. 2, February, 1969, p. 44.

6. John Tierney, "Do You Suffer From Decision Fatigue?" *New York Times*, August 17, 2011.

7. Jeanne E. Arnold, Anthony P. Graesch, Enzo Ragazzini, and Elinor Ochs, *Life at Home in the Twenty-First Century: 32 Familieis Open Their Doors,* (UCLA Cotsen Institute of Archaeology Press, 2012).

8. "Vanguard Total Stock Market Index Fund Summary Prospectus," Vanguard, last modified April 27, 2017, https://www.vanguard.com/pub/Pdf/sp85.pdf.

9. "Vanguard Total Stock Market Index Fund Summary Prospectus," Vanguard, last modified April 27, 2017, https://www.vanguard.com/pub/Pdf/sp85.pdf.

10. "Multilevel Marketing." Federal Trade Commission (website), July 2016, https://www.consumer.ftc.gov/articles/0065-multilevel-marketing.

11. "Have You Ever Tried to Sell a Diamond?," accessed January 3, 2017, http://www.edwardjayepstein.com/diamond_print.htm.

12. "What a WV Smoker Spends on Cigarettes in a Lifetime" West Virginia Department of Health and

Human Services, last modified April 2011, http://www.wvdhhr.org/bph/hsc/pubs/other/spendingoncigarettes/summary_what_a_smoker_spends_on_cigs_110422.pdf.

13. Gary Taubes, *Why We Get Fat and What to Do About It,* (New York: Knopf, 2010).

14. "Curse of the lottery winner," ABC News, last modified March 11, 2007, http://abcnews.go.com/GMA/curse-lottery-winners/story?id=2941589.

15. "Report On Average Rates For Cable Programming Service And Equipment", released June 7, 2013, Federal Communications Commission, https://apps.fcc.gov/edocs_public/attachmatch/DA-13-1319A1.pdf.

Photo © 2015 Susan Wang Photography

ABOUT THE AUTHOR

Anita Dhake is the author of the *Power of Thrift* blog, where she journals her attempts at crossing off life bucket list items. She slayed item #7, "retire early," at the age of thirty-three and was subsequently featured in Forbes, Crain's Chicago Business, and the ABA Journal. She was also interviewed on Michaela Pereira's show on the HLN Network and WGN Morning News, allowing her to cross off Life Bucket List item #16, "be on TV once," twice.

Dhake graduated from the University of Chicago law school in 2009 and quit lawyering in 2015. She now travels and attacks other bucket list items, spreading the word on how awesome life can be.

Follow her musings online at *thepowerofthrift.com*. She talks about more ways to save, plans operations, discusses travel, records her mom's recipes, contemplates happiness and shares whatever other nonsense flits through her brain.

Made in United States
North Haven, CT
08 October 2022